THE PURPOSE OF THE GOSPEL

By
G. CAMPBELL MORGAN, D.D.

WIPF & STOCK · Eugene, Oregon

Wipf and Stock Publishers
199 W 8th Ave, Suite 3
Eugene, OR 97401

The Purpose of the Gospel
Sermons
By Morgan, G. Campbell
Copyright©1934 by Morgan, G. Campbell
ISBN 13: 978-1-62032-765-4
Publication date 12/1/2012
Previously published by Zondervan, 1934

G. Campbell Morgan Reprint Series

Foreword

IF IT is true that the measure of a person's greatness is their influence, not only on his own time but on future generations, G. Campbell Morgan must be regarded as a great person. His greatness is seen not only in the wide impact of his ministry on both sides of the Atlantic, but in the fact that his books are still read and studied sixty-five years after his death. Named one of the ten greatest preachers of the twentieth-century by the contributing board of *Preaching* magazine, Morgan made the Bible a new and living book not only to the congregations who listened to him, but the vast multitude of persons who read his books.

Fox sixty-seven years Morgan preached and taught the Scriptures and served churches in England and the United States. What is remarkable is that his commentaries and expositions of the Bible still speak to persons of a new millennium. There have been many changes in the world since he faithfully preached and taught the Scriptures, but the wide appeal of his books testify to the timelessness of his message.

Although he held pastorates in the Congregational and Presbyterian denominations, he had an ecumenical appeal to persons of all denominations and traditions. The mystic

Thomas á Kempis once wrote, "He to whom the eternal word speaks is delivered from many opinions." In one of his sermons, he referred to the words of Amos that there would be a famine for hearing the word of God (Amos 8:11). The timeless work of G. Campbell Morgan addresses that hunger, as his books enable his readers to get beyond opinions to the living Word.

Wipf and Stock Publishers have rendered a great gift to the religious world in reprinting dozens of Morgan's books. This growing collection makes his books more available, so that readers have an option other than searching the internet for used, and often expensive, copies. Among this collection is the classic *The Great Physician* and commentaries on the Gospel of Matthew and John. Persons seeking a living faith and a meaningful encounter with God would profit from reading any of these Morgan books.

Near the end of his ministry, in a sermon entitled "But One Thing," Morgan commented on how Portugal changed the words of a coin after Christopher Columbus discovered America. No longer did the inscription say, *Ne Plus Ultra* (nothing more beyond) but *Plus Ultra* (more beyond). It is the hope of the G. Campbell Morgan Trust that the reprinting of these books will bring readers to the "more beyond," and an even deeper encounter with the Word in Scripture.

THE MORGAN TRUST
Richard L. Morgan
Howard C. Morgan
John C. Morgan

CONTENTS

The Purpose of the Gospel	7
Romans 1:7.	
The Effect of the Gospel	20
Romans 8:1.	
The Appeal of the Gospel	32
Romans 12:1, 2.	
The Call of Christ	44
Matthew 11:28.	
The Coming Glory	55
Titus 2:11-13.	
"Jacob's Wrestling"	64
Genesis 32:24.	
Does the Nation Consider?	81
Isaiah 1:3.	
The Remnant of God's People	93
Isaiah 1:9.	
Conscience	105

THE PURPOSE OF THE GOSPEL

Romans 1:17.

"Therein is revealed a righteousness of God."

That is the text. In order to an intelligent apprehension of it, let us read again its immediate context as we find it in the paragraph beginning at the fourteenth verse; "I am debtor both to Greeks and to barbarians, both to the wise and to the foolish. So, as much as in me is, I am ready to preach the Gospel; for it is the power of God unto salvation, for every one that believeth; to the Jew first, and also to the Greek. For therein is revealed a righteousness of God by faith; as it is written, But the righteous shall live by faith." That reading interprets for us the first word of the text, the word "therein." The reference is to the Gospel. In the Gospel, says the Apostle, a righteousness of God is revealed. Therein righteousness has an apocalypse, an unveiling, a revelation. This particular verb, to unveil, and its cognate substantives are all reserved in the New Testament to describe acts of God. Whenever we read of a revelation, it is a revelation by God; whenever we read in the New Testament of something unveiled, it is God who unveils. Moreover, the verbs and substantives alike are reserved to describe acts of God which result in making clear to the vision of man something that otherwise would be obscure. In this sense the word "revealed" is used in the text.

The idea, then, is that in the Gospel God has revealed before the eyes of men His righteousness. Now it is perfectly patent that the thought is not that God has revealed the idea of righteousness in the Gospel. Man knew very much about righteousness apart from the Gospel. The idea is revealed in nature; and clearly revealed in the law. The declaration is rather that in the Gospel a righteousness is unveiled as at the disposal of unrighteous men. So far as the purpose of the Gospel is concerned, that is its deepest note. Its nature, its power, and its terms are other phases of the great theme. There is no reference here to its nature. This is not a declaration concerning its power, though the text follows closely upon the declaration of that power. Nothing is said here of the terms upon which men may avail themselves of it, though that follows immediately. In this brief phrase we have simply a statement of the purpose of the Gospel. Therein is unveiled a righteousness of God.

There are two matters, then, that have to be considered; first, the idea of righteousness; secondly, and principally, the Gospel unveiling of righteousness.

Righteousness is a commonplace word, and, may I not add, suggests a commonplace idea. By that I do not mean to say that either the word or the idea lack richness and value, but that they are familiar. They are no longer the words merely of the Christian Church. The idea conveyed by the word works powerfully in the minds and character of many who do not claim any relationship to vital Christianity. We are always in danger of taking some idea which is perfectly patent and familiar, and devitalising it by using it in wrong connections and in wrong applications. Therefore, we shall not be wasting time in considering in the simplest way what this great word "righteousness" really means.

Our own Teutonic word "righteousness" is an abstract noun, derived from the word "righteous". Righteous, originally an adjective, also an adverb, sometimes now a substantive, simply means the right way or fashion of doing things. The word is really a corruption of the word "rightwise". It was only in the sixteenth century that the form righteous was adopted. This word "righteous" or "rightwise", then, comes from the word "right". That is a common Teutonic word — one dare not call it Anglo-Saxon, for it belongs to all the Teutonic languages in some form. The word "right" was originally an adjective, which became presently a noun, having close relationship to the Latin — rectus — meaning straight. There we reach bedrock. Right means straight.

Now, what is straightness? A straight line has been accurately described as the shortest way from any given point to any other. Rightness, in the realm of moral ideas and of spiritual truth, is straightness; that is, that which is not crooked, not twisted, having no circumlocution. Rightness, then, is conformity to a standard.

In the Greek word we have exactly the same idea, only under a different figure. Dikaiosune is an abstract noun, and is derived from Dikaios, an adjective or adverb derived from Dike. A simple word used to describe right as self-evident. This word is closely allied with a word — Deiknus — that means simply to be seen, that is, that which is clear, that which is shown, that about which there can be no question. Thus the Greek word reaches right down to elemental things, and suggests that right is the thing that is plain, a fact concerning which there can be no further argument.

Thus both words stand for the same idea; truth, justice, equity; that which squares with a moral consciousness, and with which a moral consciousness must square itself.

THE STANDARD OF RIGHTEOUSNESS

But we must go further, for the insufficiency of what we have already done is patent. We have referred to a moral realm, but we have not been introduced to it by our discussion of the word. If righteousness is straightness, the direct connection between two given points, what are the two points? Until we have defined them we have no moral or spiritual value in the word at all. If righteousness is conformity to that which is clear, self-evident, what is that? If we say that righteousness is conformity to a standard, what is the standard? If in our discussion of the word we have spoken of moral consciousness, we necessarily begin again to ask questions. Does righteousness create the standard of moral consciousness? Or does the moral consciousness create the standard of righteousness?

All that leads us to the recognition of the fact that when we use the word "righteousness" in religion, when we use it in the moral realm, we are implicating something which we are not naming. We are implicating a standard. We must have the standard. We suppose two points, and that they are defined; and until these are defined we do not understand what is meant by straightness as between the two. We are implicating the idea that there are certain things which have been made perfectly clear, that is, we are implicating the idea of law. Therefore, the idea inevitably implicates some one final authority which sets the standard up. It implicates a judge, who decides the points which regulate the straightness of the line, who utters the law which is to be the patent self-evident thing. That final One is God Himself. He declares the true lines of conduct by revelation to men of His own will, because finally in the eternal necessity of His own nature, He is the right, and right for man is conditioned by what He is.

God's great business which humanity is to demonstrate to the individual soul, and ultimately to the race, His own righteousness. That is the meaning of the great call in the prophecy of Isaiah; "Come now, and let us reason together, saith the Lord." Man is right, and therefore righteous in proportion as he thinks God's thoughts and agrees with them; in proportion as he feels the Divine emotion and answers its impulse; in proportion as all his choices are based upon the choosing of the will of God; in proportion as every action of his life is co-operation with the Divine activity. In other words, a man in full and final fellowship with God, in thought, mind, choice, and action, is a righteous man.

THE FRUITS OF RIGHTEOUSNESS

What, then, does righteousness mean to the individual? Complete joy, resulting from perfect peace, consequent upon rightness with God. If a man is right with God, all his life mastered by the perfect and acceptable will of God, he is at peace, and finds fulness of joy in the fulfillment of life. This is eternal life; righteousness, the fundamental condition; peace, the inevitable result; joy, the glad experience.

What, then, is social righteousness? The perfect human society, in which there are no inequalities, no injustice, no tyrannies, no lusts for power, which march through rapine and bloodshed to an unholy throne. Human society made up of righteous society; a society of infinite and abiding peace; a society of song, never ribald or obscene; a society of laughter, never frivolous like the crackling of thorns under a pot; a glad and holy society full of heavenly joy.

In the Gospel there is an unveiling of a righteousness of God, which He places at the disposal of men. That such an unveiling is needful, implicates hiding. That which is hidden is not a concept, but an experience. Therefore the idea is that man is unable to be right. He knows what right is, but has never been able to find his way into rightness or righteousness. Christianity is a religion for men who lack righteousness. If that is a blunt way to put it, I will amend the statement, and express it in the words of our Lord Himself; "I came not to call the righteous, but sinners to repentance." If there be a man who by birth and development and experience is righteous, Christ has no message for him in the Gospel.

THE UNVEILING OF RIGHTEOUSNESS

In the argument of this letter, Paul elaborately and conclusively claims that all men are sinners. He begins with the Gentiles, drawing a sharp distinction between the Jews and all other peoples. He declares that these had held down the truth in unrighteousness. He affirms that God's revelation of righteousness came first through nature. He had never left Himself without witness that He Himself was righteous. The invisible things of God, the spiritual and moral realities, were clearly revealed through the things that He created; through creation His power and His Divinity were manifested.

That declaration of Paul is in perfect consonance with the latest findings of scientific investigation. That is exactly the point at which the scientist reverently halts. He prosecutes his investigations in the realm of nature, and always at last comes to the last word, to a dead wall, to a cloud of mystery; and then he tells us that all he has any right to say as the result of his investigation is that at the back of all natural phenomena there "is a double-faced somewhat." He finds through creation intelligence and power working in a strange and wonderful co-operation.

That is exactly what Paul said. But, then, Paul declared that when men find that in nature, their true action is that of venturing out upon it, that they ought to say God, and to relate their lives to Him through the laws revealed in nature.

There I want to turn aside for a moment. Some men say to-day, "We do not care about religion. We worship nature. We go into the country to worship nature." On investigation it will generally be found that such men walk far enough into the country to stop at an hotel and have dinner! If a man really worships nature, he gives himself up on it, he follows it, he lets it lead him, he observes its laws. If he will do so, after a while, he will find that righteousness emerges; in every flower that blossoms in the field, in every tree that grows in the forest, the law of righteousness obtains. If in these there shall be for any reason deflection from the straight line of law, destruction and punishment inevitably follow. The proclamation of the whole realm of nature is that God is righteous. As Paul said, these men instead of finding their way through nature to God, halt in nature, and make gods of birds and beasts, and of their own evil passions. Thus tarrying in the realm of creation, they become corrupt, and God gives them up to their own choices.

To these very men, to the very men who have not obeyed the revelation of rightness in nature, and consequently are in themselves unrighteous to men lacking righteousness, in the Gospel God has given an apocalypse of righteousness at their disposal.

Proceeding with his argument, Paul turned to the Jew. With that swift sharp sentence, "Who art thou, O man, that judgest," he began to deal with the men of his own nation, of his own religion, of his own birthright and blood. He told them that they also were unrighteous men. They boasted in the law. They boasted that they had been made the depository of a distinct revelation as to life. They boasted in the fact that God had interpreted righteousness to them in words that arranged the condition of all their life. They had the oracles. To such, said the apostle, have you kept your law? Have you obeyed your oracles? Are you living in accordance with the law in which you make your boast? If not, then they also lacked righteousness.

At the close of his argument as to the necessity for the Gospel, Paul summarized everything by declaring that "Every mouth must be stopped and all the world become guilty before God," for "All have sinned and come short of the glory of God." All men have failed to realize the divine ideal, failed to be in their own lives what they were intended to be; failed of life's beauty, failed of its glory, failed of its excellence.

Moreover, it is not only true that men lack righteousness, it is also true that they are not able to be righteous. The choices they have made have reacted upon them, so that they cannot, if they would, be righteous. In the course of this letter, in a great passage full of the memory of his own poignant agony, Paul tells the story of the experience of such a human soul: "When I would do good, evil is present with me." "I delight in the law of God after the inward man." I see its beauty, but I cannot realize it. Woe is me! "O wretched man that I am! who shall deliver me?" That is the cry of the human soul illuminated as to righteousness, but lacking it as an experience conscious of a paralysis which makes it unable to realize the idea.

In the Gospel, God had unveiled a righteousness which is at the disposal of all such souls. Twice already I have said that this is not the unveiling of the idea of righteousness, that the apostle here did not mean that in the Gospel the conception of righteousness was given to men. But while this is so it is nevertheless true that in the unveiling of righteousness in the Gospel the idea and the concept have their most perfect interpretation. Men discover righteousness in nature, but what that righteousness really is is revealed perfectly in the Gospel. Men knew righteousness by the law, but the full and final content of the righteousness of which they were made aware by the law only came to them in the Gospel. There are three stages of revelation. Righteousness revealed through nature is misty, definite, but undefined. Righteousness revealed through law consists of terms and words and commandments, explanations and interpretations of the self-same mystery of Nature, so that men might know how to order their lives. Finally, righteousness unveiled in the Gospel. The righteousness which is unveiled in the Gospel is not a compromise, it is not a second best. The idea of the text, the idea of the

Gospel, is not that seeing man lacks pure righteousness, God accepts something less than the best from him. Nay, verily! The righteousness unveiled in the Gospel in the very righteousness of God, in all its wonder, in all its glory, in all its awe-inspiring truth, and in all its compelling grace. In the Gospel we discover that righteousness in God is not Law only, it is Love; it is not government merely, it is grace; it is not truth alone, it is compassion working so as to enable the untrue to become true.

RIGHTEOUSNESS SEEN IN CHRIST

The Gospel is first the proclamation of truth concerning a Person, a Person described by the holy apostle as the Holy and Righteous One. So that, if we want to know what righteousness is, we do not go to Nature; we do not go to the Law; we look at God's Man, at Incarnate Righteousness.

Looking at Him, and remembering those very simple definitions with which we began, we see in Him what a straight line really means. The two points are those of God and the soul. Righteousness is direct, immediate, unbroken, unswerving communication between these two. In Jesus we see what righteousness is. As a boy He said, "I must be in the things of My Father." Even His mother, according to the flesh, must be made to stand on one side, that His soul might take a straight line to God. Said He in manhood, "I speak nothing from Myself. What My Father gives Me, that I speak." Thus all human opinions were discounted. His ear was open to listen to the voice of God. Again He said, "I do nothing of Myself. What My Father commands Me, that I do." Thus all personal planning and arranging were abandoned. Here was a Man who, in the very beauty of His manhood, exemplified for evermore the unutterable glory of that against which men in their sinfulness are for evermore rebelling, submission to authority.

Or, if we take the other idea of what righteousness is, that it is self-evident truth, we behold it perfectly exemplified in Him. Said John, "We behold His glory, full of grace and truth." Said Jesus, "I am the truth." His life was for ever in harmony with the underlying essential facts and truths of the universe. That is the story of the life of Jesus; so that all its infinite harmonies, its subtlest melodies, found expression in the carpenter's shop, in the highways and the byways of Judea and Galilee, as He talked with publicans and sinners whom other men held in contempt, and evoked from them music that gladdened the angels and made heaven richer. That is righteousness.

For Him moral standards were those ways of life that ensured happiness. His Moral Manifesto, that great ethical utterance, began with the statement, Happy! are the poor in spirit. Eight times over, making the perfect octave, the music of intended happiness rings and vibrates at the opening of His ethical code. That was His idea of morality. Morality is not something stern and hard. The way of morality, according to Jesus, is the highway of joy, it is the highway to the condition of life which blossoms into infinite beauty and lives itself out in multiplication of happiness. That is righteousness according to Jesus.

But there is another and a deeper note. When He came to fulfill righteousness, he came into an unrighteous world. Now what is the experience of righteousness in an unrighteous world? What is the deepest note, its richest content, its most poignant glory? For answer let us listen to Him again. He was at the beginning of His public ministry. Behind Him were the strong years of righteousness in the Carpenter's Shop. He stood upon the banks of the Jordan and looked into the eyes of the last of the long line of illustrious Hebrew prophets, John, and asked for baptism. John looked into His eyes, and said, with keen intuition, "I have need to be baptized of Thee and cometh Thou to me?" By that John meant to say; "Mine is a baptism of repentance; Thou hast nothing of which to repent; mine is a baptism for sinning men; Thou art not a sinning man." To me there is nothing more radiantly wonderful in all the recorded words of Christ than what He answered John on the threshold of His public ministry: "Suffer it to be so now, for thus it becometh us to fulfil all righteousness." It was as though He had said: John, the very thing against which you are making your protest is the final fact in righteousness in such a world as this; that the Sinless should identify Himself with the sinning, that the pure should take the place of the impure, that the Man who has nothing to repent should gather into His own heart, and take responsibility for, sins that He never committed, and that He should die to deliver others. That is righteousness. That is what the righteousness of God does in a world like ours. Presently some one wrote about Him that startling thing, so often carelessly read, and yet so stupendous in its unveiling of truth, "He was crowned with glory and honour, that He might taste death for every man." The statement is not that He was crowned with glory and honour because He tasted death. It is that God conferred upon Himself the high dignity of tasting death for every man. This is what He Himself said: "Therefore doth the Father love Me, because I lay down My life . . . . This command-

THE PURPOSE OF THE GOSPEL

ment received I from My Father." In the Gospel unveiling of righteousness we learn that God's awful holiness is finally of such a nature that in the presence of man's lack, God suffers and dies that man may live. That is the Gospel unveiling of righteousness.

RIGHTEOUSNESS AVAILABLE

This leads us to the final meaning of the text. By reason of that fact, righteousness is available to men. Look on to His death upon the Cross. There His righteousness is placed at the disposal of man for his forgiveness. No man is forgiven upon the basis of pity. God forgives a man because His righteousness is vindicated, and vindicated by His own activity in sacrifice and in death. By His resurrection from among the dead, righteousness is placed at the disposal of man for the cleansing of his nature, and for his enoblement. By His ascension to the right hand of the Father, and the consequent coming of the Spirit at Pentecost, righteousness is placed at the disposal of man for growth and development and for service.

That is the meaning of the Gospel. Nothing short of righteousness. But infinitely more, Peace! And Joy! are also in the Gospel. They are rooted here. There is no peace, and there is no ultimate or perfect joy, for the unrighteous soul. So God's Gospel comes, not to offer man imperfect joy, not to offer a man unworthy peace, but to proclaim the possibility of righteousness. So the Gospel is the power of God unto salvation, for individuals, for society for nations! There is no way into righteousness but through the Gospel. We may see its gleaming glory in Nature, we may hear its marvellous requirements in the Law, but in the Gospel alone we receive its power. Therein is revealed a righteousness of God.

THE EFFECT OF THE GOSPEL

Romans 8:1.

"There is, therefore, now no condemnation to them that are in Christ Jesus."

In our previous meditation we considered the purpose of the Gospel as it is set forth in the words, "Therein is revealed a righteousness of God." In the words of our present text, found at the very heart and centre of the letter, we have a statement of the effect produced by the Gospel in the case of those who believe its message and receive the righteousness which is therein revealed; "There is therefore now no condemnation to them that are in Christ Jesus."

This is a fittingly smooth and accurate translation of what the apostle wrote. It nevertheless loses some of the force of the original, which is exclamatory and explosive. As Paul wrote the statement, it contained no verb. It is not a complete sentence. The "is" and the "are" which we have in our translation have been introduced to create smoothness and to make a complete sentence, but in the text the statement opens with an emphatic negative. "No condemnation!" So emphatic is the negative that we might render it with exact accuracy, "No sort of condemnation!" It is the glad exultant cry of a soul apprehending the fullest meaning of what the Gospel has wrought for men. It is closely connected in the letter with the cry of the soul in its agony. It is indeed part of the reply thereto. The word of which we must think, by way of introduction, is the word "therefore." The "therefore"

THE EFFECT OF THE GOSPEL

of the text shows that the statement is rooted in that whole apostolic argument concerning justification.

That being recognized, there are two things which we have to consider. First, the idea, and realm of condemnation which were in the apostle's mind as he wrote; and secondly, and of course principally, the sphere and experience of no condemnation in which he rejoiced, as he wrote the words of this text.

What is meant by condemnation? What is involved in the idea? The simple meaning of the word "condemnation" is that of being under adverse sentence. It is peculiarly a forensic term. When we speak of condemnation, we are thinking of a charge that has been made, of evidence that has been heard, of a verdict which has been found, and of a sentence which has been pronounced. Condemnation stands in direct opposition to justification. Both words belong to the law courts.

The word condemnation had a distinctly criminal association. It was always judicial, but sometimes it applied to cases that could not be described as criminal. Deissmann has given us illustrations of the fact that at the time when Paul was using the word it had a civil application; it referred not merely to criminal guilt and sentence, but also to penalties resting upon a man because he had failed to fulfil obligations even when he was not guilty of any crime. Deissmann suggests that we might render the word "legal burden." Condemnation, then, is the condition of being under sentence for failure, either wilfully, or without the will having played any part in the failure.

It is an interesting fact that, whereas the verb is found again and again in the New Testament, this actual substantive, this abstract noun, only occurs therein three times, and they are all in this letter. The other two cases are in the fifth chapter. There, in the sixteenth verse, we read: "Not as though one that sinned, so is the gift; for the judgment came of one unto condemnation, but the free gift came of many trespasses unto justification." In that verse the two words, condemnation and justification, stand opposite to each other in their true and accurate contrast. In the eighteenth verse we read: "So then, as through one trespass the judgment came unto all men to condemnation; even so through one act of righteousness the free gift came unto all men to justification of life." Again, the two words stand confronting each other in their true and proper contrast. In our text Paul does not employ the word justification, but he refers to the fact which negatives condemnation; "No more condemnation therefore to them that are in Christ Jesus."

In order to understand what Paul means by condemnation, we must remind ourselves of the line of argument that he has been following. In that argument he claims that every man stands under a sentence of God, resulting from a verdict which the law has found against him; and that the soul, the conscience of man, is in agreement with that verdict and with that sentence. The realm of condemnation, as revealed in the apostolic argument, may thus be stated. The soul is under the condemnation of God. The soul is under the condemnation of the law of God. The soul is self-condemned. Condemnation rests upon more than the sentence of God, on the verdict of the law, on the consent of conscience. This threefold condemnation may be described as racial condemnation, legal condemnation, personal condemnation.

Racial condemnation is the sentence of God against

THE EFFECT OF THE GOSPEL

failure whether criminal or no. In the line of his argument Paul has summed up all under sin, has declared that every mouth must be stopped, and all the world become guilty before God. He shows that there are sins and sins. There are men who have sinned after the similitude of Adam's transgression, and there are those who have sinned against the light of conscience. In every case men have sinned, and so are under the sentence of God.

Legal condemnation is the sentence of the law against rebellion, whether rebelling be against the law as written, or against the principle of right and truth manifest in all creation. This is wholly criminal. A man is under the condemnation of the eternal righteousness of God, if he has failed, even though the element of wilful sin has not entered into his failure. A man is under the condemnation of the law, if he has broken its requirements or has refused to walk in the light which has come to him from nature.

CONSCIENCE AS A JUDGE

Personal condemnation is the final fact. The conscience of man, though it may be seared, hardened, twisted, never perishes; and that conscience agrees with the verdict of the law and the sentence of God. That is the sense of sin which found expression in the words: O wretched man that I am! Here we have the exact description of what every soul feels when brought into the light of divine things, and the apprehension of spiritual truth. No soul escapes such moments of awakening, when the reality of the spiritual becomes the supreme impression. The impression may be refused. Men may turn away from it, they may so harden themselves that presently it ceases to make any appeal to them, and they may even become guilty of the unutterable folly of laughing at their own serious impressions. But every human soul, sooner or later, is brought to the consciousness of the spiritual, not always and not often by intellectual argument or apprehension, but constantly by emotional intelligence and insight. How varied are the means by which God breaks through upon the soul. Have any of you ever come, in some moment of exceptional circumstances, to the consciousness of the spirituality of your being? I think most of us do so sooner or later.

I shall never forget one brief five minutes in my life when, apart from the question of religion, I became conscious of my spiritual self, and felt my body to be a clod and a hindrance. It was on a day of terrific explosion in New York City, when by the merest hand's breadth I escaped being blown to atoms. I went back to the hotel and climbed up four flights of stairs, the lift being destroyed, to see if my loved ones were safe. I felt the weight of my body, and came to acute spiritual consciousness. In that moment of spiritual consciousness truth about God and the soul flashed before me. That is what the man tells you who nearly loses his life by drowning; all the facts of life set in the light of the spiritual, break in upon such a man. That, I think, happens in some way to every man sooner or later. It is God breaking through. It has happened to thousands of men in the trenches. As surely as it has happened, and those men, in the very hour and article of death have flung themselves upon the compassion of God, they have been forgiven and received into light. They are not in heaven because they were patriots. Salvation by patriotism is a very dangerous heresy. They are there because they flung themselves upon the mercy of God for

> 'Twixt the stirrup and the ground,
> Salvation sought, salvation found;

is a great and true philosophy.

When the soul is awakened to spiritual things, it looks for God and knows its condemnation. Then all the trivalities of life stand out in their true perspective, and the most trivial thing is seen to be mighty in its bearing upon the infinite order, and upon the disorder of the soul. When a man knows that he is less than the man God meant him to be, he knows that he is under the condemnation of God; when a man knows that he has broken the law, refused to yield to the truth as it has broken forth upon his soul from any point, he knows that he stands condemned in the moral universe. That is the realm of condemnation. That is the background, dark and sinister and terrible, as every soul knows when it has ever come face to face with the fact of sin, and felt the poignant agony of it.

"IN CHRIST JESUS."

But it is only the background. Now we appreciate the fact that there is no verb in the text. It is rather the glad, exultant cry of a soul; "No sort of condemnation now therefore to them who are in Christ Jesus." To them who are in Christ Jesus, the law's verdict is changed, God's sentence is revoked, the soul's burden is rolled away.

The sphere in which men find this experience is described in the pregnant phrase: "In Christ Jesus." When we inquire what this means we go back to the fifth chapter, where we find three phrases which will help us. The first is in the first verse: "Justified by faith." The second is in the second verse: "Access by faith into grace." The third is in the tenth verse: "Saved through His life." Those are in Christ Jesus who are justified by faith, who have access into grace, who are being saved through His life.

"Justified by faith." Faith is return to obedience and so to righteousness; Faith is obedience; faith is trust; faith is abandonment to truth, with a commensurate activity of the will in the direction of that abandonment. I stand under condemnation for I have failed; I stand under condemnation for I have broken the law. God unveils in front of me a righteousness at my disposal in Christ Jesus. He says that it is at my disposal. He asks me to believe, to trust Him, and when he does so, He is uttering a new command. I have broken all His commandments. I will venture upon the declaration of God. I will trust my soul with all its guilt to Christ Jesus. When I utter that "I will trust," I am obeying the law, I am returning to the principle of righteousness. That is the first thing. Thus God by His own act justifies the soul. Justification is infinitely more than forgiveness. It is making the soul not guilty, which was guilty. That cannot be done in any court of law in this world. No act of man can cancel the guilt of his fellow man in the matter of human inter-relationships. Justice and mercy can never agree together in any earthly court of law. If the prisoner be arraigned before the judges, the trial will proceed and the jury will bring in their verdict. If that verdict be "Not Guilty", they are not justifying the prisoner. They are declaring that he never ought to be there. He is not guilty. That is justice, but it is not justification. If the prisoner be guilty, then the sentence is pronounced, and the pris-

THE EFFECT OF THE GOSPEL

oner is condemned. Then a plea may be put in of extenuating circumstances. Let that plea of extenuating circumstances obtain. Now what will the court do? Extend mercy to the prisoner. Then the mercy of the court sets the prisoner free and violates justice; for the moment an earthly court extends mercy to a guilty soul, the principle of justice is violated. But when God justifies, He extends mercy to the guilty souls, but He does not violate justice. He extends mercy to the guilty soul because every demand of infinite and holy justice has been met in the mystery of the dying of His Son, and so He declares that the guilty soul is no longer guilty. The very guilt is cancelled and the wrong is put away, and the justified soul passes out free from guilt and divine condemnation through the one act of obedience and faith. The infinite and fathomless resources of the Atonement of God in Christ are placed at the disposal of the trusting soul. That is being justified by faith.

"Access into grace." The soul in Christ Jesus stands in divine favour. God accepts the soul that He has justified, so that it now stands, not merely uncondemned by His righteousness, but welcomed by His holiness. Holiness is at the very heart of grace. Grace never violates holiness.

What is it to stand in grace? It is to be in favour with God, and this means the right of access to Him, which the child has to the father, which the most intimate friend has to the most intimate friend. It means far more than being at peace with God, it means far more than being justified in the sense of standing before God free from guilt. I am at peace with King George V. I have no quarrel with His Majesty and he has none with me. I am not breaking his law. I am not condemned. But I am not in favour. I constantly pass Buckingham Palace, but I never call. But the soul justified by faith in Christ is admitted to favour with God. The soul calls at the royal palace whenever it so desires. Nay, it dwells in the royal place and sits at the royal table as a child of the king.

"In Christ Jesus" is standing in favour, and the soul that was condemned — the condemnation being put away by an act of justification which has in it the element of justice and purity and holiness — passes into the realm of grace and is in favour.

"Saved through His life." This final phrase refers to the process by which justification is being demonstrated in the life. The verdict and the sentence of God upon the soul are that the soul is clear from guilt and admitted to favour. But the soul is still weak, faltering. Now by the application of the infinite values of the Cross and the Resurrection of our Lord that soul is being saved in His life. The mind travels back to an historic story of the Old Testament, and it suggests an illustration. When King David came into His kingdom he said, "Is there any left of the house of Saul that I may show some kindness for Jonathan's sake?" There was one found of the house of Saul, Mephibosheth, a cripple, lame on both feet. And David said, "Send for him and bring him to me." David gave Mephibosheth, the cripple, a place at the royal table; and mark the significance of the declaration, His feet were under the table. The royal guests assembled, and Mephibosheth sat there, his imperfection not seen, because it was hidden under the king's table. For a little way that is an illustration, and then it breaks down. We also sit at the king's table, not perfect even yet; but we sit there, justified, in favour, admitted of grace to the hospitality of the king. There the figure breaks down, for David the king could not heal Mephibosheth of his limitation. But we are being saved in His life. The atrophied powers are being renewed. In Christ Jesus we are being fashioned anew in spirit and in mind. Ere He finish His work with us the very body of our limitation will be fashioned anew like unto the body of His glory.

THE FRUITS OF "NO CONDEMNATION"

Let us then consider briefly the experience of no condemnation. In doing so we must call to mind Paul's illustrations as they are found in the preceding chapters. The first has to do with the race. Adam was the head of a race. Christ is the head of a race. The second is in the realm of mystery. Sin is a master. Righteousness, that is Christ, is a master. His last is in the realm of the marriage relationship. The law and sinful passion revealed by it was the bridegroom of the failing soul. Christ becomes the Bridegroom of the soul being saved. These are the illustrations that at last led up to this glad and exultant cry. Christ is at the head of a new race. Christ is the Master over that new race. Christ is the Bridegroom into fellowship with whom all souls pass who are made members of that race. These, then, are the phases of the experience of no condemnation.

Christ is the racial head. The soul which is justified knows a transference of relationship. I am linked by nature to the man who first sinned. In Christ I find a new relationship. In the act of justification I am brought by God into actual and active relationship with Him. I appropriate a new heredity. The Gospel says to me: It is perfectly true that your sinning is the result of your relationship with the federal head of the race. But in Christ you enter upon a relationship of power, which cancels all the forces that are operating within you and driving you to sin. So that I am no longer under condemnation because I am a member of a sinning race, for in Christ I am a member of a ransomed and redeemed race; and ranson and redemption mean ability not to sin.

That carries with it, involved within it, the idea of the transference of authority. A new loyalty springs up in the life. Sin no longer reigns. Righteousness reigns—that is, Christ reigns. That does not necessarily mean that the man who received the gift of life never sins again; but it does mean that sin does not reign. We have a perfect right to quote the words, "And if we sin, we have an advocate with the Father"; but when we do so we must not begin there. That is not the first thing that John wrote. He wrote: "My little children, these things write I unto you, that ye sin not, and if any man sin . . ." We must not make John's "If" a license for sin. By the infinite grace of God, we may claim the advocacy of Christ, but we may not make that fact a license for sinning. Sin does not reign. There is no condemnation, because we do not live under the mastery of sin, but under the mastery of righteousness.

Finally, the relationship with Christ is that He becomes the bridegroom of the soul. This means transference of fellowship. Life is no longer in fellowship with sinful passions; but the heart being "joined to another, even to Him that was raised from the dead," then the new life of the Lord becomes the law of life.

This is the first and fundamental effect of the Gospel. It is the first phase of the righteousness unveiled. It is justification. All the things of which I have tried to speak are summarized in that word of the apostle. No sort of condemnation therefore to them in Christ Jesus! This is not an altitude to which the soul can climb. It is an altitude to which the soul is lifted by the grace of God. It is immediate. In the moment in which the soul trusts, believes, obeys, it passes from condemnation.

God no longer condemns. We are "translated into the kingdom of the Son of His love," and we may employ the words of the prophet of long ago: "Oh, Jehovah, I will give thanks unto Thee, for Thou wast angry with me, but Thine anger is turned away, for Jehovah is become my salvation."

The law no longer condemns because Christ has expiated our failure and undertaken for our perfecting. Christ has made satisfaction forever to the law. He will see to it that in the case of all trusting souls, that is, every requirement shall at last be met and fulfilled in righteousness.

Conscience no longer condemns. It will remain with us to the end, causing us to remember with sorrow how we broke the law and how we did despite to the Spirit of Grace. It will talk to us to the end of the unutterable folly of the past. But it no longer condemns, because we are trusting in His grace and yielding to the forces of His life.

That experience of no condemnation becomes the very inspiration which energizes us for response to all His will. The second phase of righteousness is progressively realized in our sanctification, but this is the fundamental blessing.

> No condemnation, O, my soul,
> 'Tis God that speaks the word!
> Perfect in comeliness art thou,
> In Christ, thy Risen Lord.

THE APPEAL OF THE GOSPEL

Romans 12:1, 2.

"I beseech you, therefore, brethren, by the mercies of God, to present your bodies a living sacrifice, holy acceptable to God, which is your reasonable service. And be not fashioned according to this world: but be ye transformed by the renewing of your mind, that ye may prove what is the good and acceptable will of God."

In the first of these meditations we considered the purpose of the Gospel as set forth in the words: "Therein is revealed a righteousness of God." In the second we considered the effect of the Gospel as declared in the words: "No condemnation now, therefore, to them in Christ Jesus." We come now to the appeal of the Gospel. The sequence of these matters is self-evident. The unveiling or righteousness is a call to faith. Faith, being exercised, the soul passes into the experience of no condemnation — that is of justification. The soul justified is appealed to in the words of our text.

The greatness of this appeal will be at once conceded. That greatness is created by its extensive and intensive notes. Extensively the appeal covers the whole ground of personality, and that in the most scientific and careful way. Intensively it deals fully and finally with every department of personality. Let these, then, be our divisions as we think of this appeal: first, its extensive outlook; and, secondly, its intensive application.

THE EXTENSIVE OUTLOOK

With regard to the extensiveness of the outlook,

let us carefully consider the concept of personality which is revealed in this verse. Paul was not technically dealing with personality, but it is evident that he had a very clear conception thereof; and the method of the appeal shows how careful that conception was. In an earlier writing of the same apostle — the first Thessalonian letter — he had defined personality when, at the close of the letter he prayed for the Thessalonian Christians that they might be preserved blameless unto the coming of the Lord. In order that he might show the full force of what he meant by being blameless, he gave a definition of personality; "That your whole spirit, soul and body be preserved entirely, without blame, unto the coming of our Lord Jesus Christ." In this Roman appeal we have the same conception, though not the same words. "Spirit" is not mentioned in this verse. The word for "mind" takes the place of the word for "soul". In the Thessalonian letter he refers to the soul (psuche), that is sentient with life; here he refers to the mind (nous), that is knowledge resident within the mind. The difference is that here he speaks of the function rather than of the organ, of consciousness rather than of capacity.

While in our text Spirit is not named, it is directly addressed. In order that this may be realized, let us indulge in a study of pronouns. First observe that the apostle addressed everything in the appeal to those whom he describes as "Brethren." He then made use of these pronouns: "You" and "Your" and "Ye"; the "Ye" being, of course, the same word "You." In the Greek New Testament we have two accusatives and two genitives; or, as we should say in our grammar, two objectives, and three possessives. These pronouns bring you into the presence of the supreme fact in personality. Notice his use of them: You, and your body, and your mind. Thus he was addressing some persons, and speaking of their possessions.

Now, all this is mechanical, but it is the very foundation of our consideration. When I was eight years old I found on the shelves of my father's library a book which some of the older people will remember, while the younger people have probably never heard of it. It was called "Todd's Lectures to Children," and, of course, that attracted the eye of a boy. I took it down and read it. One thing fastened itself on my mind, and I have never forgotten it, or lost the power of it. Dr. Todd said in one of his lectures that parents ought not to teach their children that they have souls. He went on to say that they should teach them they have bodies. There is no doubt that Dr. Todd was right. If we teach a child that it has a soul, we put the principle emphasis of personality upon the body, and the child thinks of itself as a body possessing a soul, which is not true. Teach a child that it has a body, and we place the principle emphasis of personality upon the soul, and the child thinks of itself as a soul possessing a body. That is what Paul did in this appeal. He said, "I beseech you." He was addressing Christians in Rome — Jews and Gentiles, for both were there — and he said: "Brethren, I beseech you that you present your bodies." You are not your bodies. The body is under control, it is not supreme, it is not essential; it is transitory, passing, perishing. I am talking to you. I beseech you, that you present your bodies. And again, I beseech you that you be not conformed to the age but transformed by the renewal of your mind. You have a mind, you have a consciousness; but it is not you, it is your possession.

THE APPEAL OF THE GOSPEL

So we reach the apostolic concept of personality. The essential fact of personality is not material; it is not mental; it is spiritual. The material is entirely necessary for this world, and will be necessary in a final state of being, when men, according to Scripture teaching, are to receive new bodies. Mental powers are essential to personality. Personality, devoid of them, is atrophied and imperfect; but it still exists. Mental powers are under the dominion of the spiritual, and that is what Paul meant when he said: I beseech you not to submit yourself to the fluctuating fashions of a passing age, but to relate yourself, by transformation, to the eternal verities.

The essential spirit possesses a body, possesses a mind, and renders a service. Thus we see the true place of the body in relation to personality. It is under the mastery of the spirit. And it is always so. Sin is never material in its genesis, though it is often so — but not always — in its expression. No sin of the flesh is ever committed that has not been commanded by the spirit. The body is always the instrument of the spirit. As Paul has shown in the course of his great argument, we can render our members instruments of sin, and place ourselves under the mastery of evil; or we can render them instruments of righteousness, and place ourselves under the mastery of Christ. So there is, in a sense in which everybody is living, a spiritual life. We now so use the word spiritual as to reserve it almost entirely for that which is pure and noble; but that is really an improper use. Every man is a spiritual man. That man is spiritual who is given over to every lust of the flesh. His spirit commands his bodily activity, even when it is blighting and blasting his being. The spirit is supreme, and the body is its possession, its instrument, and therefore it can be presented upon the altar — either of demons or Deity; given over to every form of lust or to the sweet mastery of love; yielded to anti-Christ or to Christ Himself.

Again, the mind is a possession of the spirit. It is the consciousness of the spirit, and it reacts upon the spirit. Here we touch the most subtle and delicate facts of personality — those of the reflex activity of the mind and of the spirit. The mind is a function and a faculty of the spirit, and yet the spirit is acted upon by that consciousness. Paul here speaks of a renewed mind, which is the mind brought under the mastery of the spirit which God has renewed by justification.

Now, what I have already said, or, rather, what has been involved in what I have said, I want to state explicitly. Those who were addressed were appealed to as free to act. Those to whom Paul wrote these words were justified; they had received the righteousness that was renewal. The spiritual life was restored to the fellowship with God. Therefore the mind had been renewed. As Paul said in writing to the Corinthians: We have the mind of Christ. The body, moreover, had been brought under, made subservient, in order to obey the commands of the spirit—made known through the renewed mind. This appeal is not made to men generally. If I say to men who are living under the mastery of the flesh, if I say to men who are living under the mastery of an evil mind: "I beseech you . . . to present your bodies a living sacrifice, holy, acceptable to God, which is your reasonable service," I am simply telling them to do what they cannot do. They are still under the mastery of sin. Paul here was not calling men to salvation; he was calling saved men to realize their salvation, to enter into it, to appropriate it, to take hold of the things already theirs in Christ Jesus, and make them living realities in their own lives. He was introducing the soul into the realm of responsibility, created not by law but by grace. Grace sets up severer responsibilities before the human soul than the law ever dreamed of. So let me repeat. The words are addressed to those whose spirits are restored to fellowship with God, whose minds have been renewed so that the whole outlook upon all life is different, and whose bodies therefore wait for the command of the restored spirit and the renewed mind — souls that are free from condemnation.

THE INTENSIVE OUTLOOK

Now, what is the appeal? We glance at it first in its extensive reaches, and then turn to consider its intensive notes and values. It is first an appeal to present the bodies living sacrifices, holy, acceptable to God. This, he says, is reasonable service. A marginal reading in the Revised Version is very suggestive; it substitutes "your spiritual worship" for "your reasonable service." There is no doubt whatever that this is the deeper meaning of the phrase. Reasonable service is rational service; and the word "service" does not mean the doing of kind deeds; it is peculiarly a word of the sanctuary; it is worship, the rendering of service to God in adoration. Bodies dedicated wholly to God are always the expression of spiritual worship, whether in the temple or in the market place, whether in the sanctuary or in the home, whether in the posture of devotion with uplifted hands or with those self-same hands busy with household duties and about the things of daily callings. Bodies presented to God perpetually are always the expressions of spirits worshipping.

Then, passing beyond that which is the outward expression of worship through the body, we come to the inward responsibility. The spirit is to be yielded to the renewed mind, and so is to cease to be conformed to the fashions of an age, and so transformed. To this we shall return presently.

In this glance at the extensive values we must notice the method of the apostolic appeal. What inspiration does he suggest as sufficient for the carrying out of this great injunction? "I beseech you by the mercies of God." What are they? I sometimes like to be reminiscent. I was looking over a sermon I made many years ago on this text, and I found I had made a list of the mercies of God, all the mercies by which He appeals. All that was true, but it missed the point of the text. The reference is really to the subject already dealt with. The words in the letter immediately preceding the text are: "O the depth of the riches both of the wisdom and the knowledge of God!" The apostle had been writing about the great salvation; God's mercy in putting righteousness at the disposal of sinful men; God's mercy in providing justification and sanctification and glorification. These are God's compassions, as they have been revealed in, and are perpetually operative through, Christ. These are the inspirations of obedience according to the appeal.

THE RENEWED MIND

Then notice again in this matter, the power he referred for obedience was that of the renewed mind, the mind changed, the new consciousness, the new outlook. This renewed mind results from life in fellowship with God. If any man be in Christ Jesus he is a new creation, and his conversation is other than it was. The whole world is changed for that man. His mind is different. His mind is renewed. His outlook upon everything is different, because his life is new. That is the power which enables a man to yield his body, and to hold himself — that is his spirit—in right relationship to God.

Notice finally the goal described. What is to be the ultimate result of it all? That you may prove what is that good and acceptable and perfect will of God. To that also we shall come back in a moment.

Now briefly, and yet I trust carefully, let us notice the intensive application of all this. We begin at the centre. The spirit is called to volitional activity as to its own condition. Mark the negative. "Be not fashioned according to this world." It is very important that we should remember that the word world here is not "Cosmos." It is "Age". Be not fashioned according to the age, but be transformed by yielding yourself up to the renewed mind that God has given you. There we have revealed the wrong and the right attitudes of spiritual being. What is the wrong attitude? Being fashioned by the age. I would like to use a word here which I think gets a little nearer to the apostolic thought than any other I know. Be not configured to the age. The suggestion of that word is very pertinent. The Christian man is never to allow himself to follow the fashions of the age. They are always changing. If there is one thing more contemptible than another from the height of spiritual elevation in human society, it is a merely fashionable man or fashionable woman. There is nothing so utterly contemptible from the spiritual height as the man or woman who is taking all the powers of spiritual life and exercising them in the interest of being correct. When doing the correct thing merely means squaring life with the fashion of an hour that is perishing, it means wearing away the rock nature and making it baseless. Then observe the positive. Be transformed. That is a great word. It is the word that was used of our Lord's Transfiguration. Be metamorphosed, be changed in essence by the renewing of your mind. Has your mind been renewed? Have you seen God in a new light? Answer the revelation, adjust yourself to that God. Have you seen men in a new way? Answer the revelation, let your life take up its true relationship with other men. Have you seen a new world? Then adjust your eye to that world, using it as not abusing it. Have you ceased to speak of sins by golden names that rob them of their devilishness because you have seen what sin really is? Then yield to that renewing of the mind, give yourself up to the light that has come. Obey and be transfigured, be changed, be metamorphosed, be lifted above the low level of the old life, and have your life related to those eternal views. The renewed mind is the new consciousness resulting from the reception of righteousness, and that is to be maintained by being yielded to. Unless we yield to it we destroy it; and if we destroy it it will be replaced by the old mind or something infinitely worse than the old mind, and all our spiritual nature will shrivel and perish and die. The touch of God upon a soul in regeneration renews the mind. The essential spirit must answer the light, or else the light will fade, and the spirit will be left again in its unutterable darkness. There is no surer way to obey the renewed mind in order that the spirit may be maintained in its fellowship with God than that which the apostle began, and to which I now come in conclusion.

"LIVING SACRIFICES"

"I beseech you therefore, by the compassions of God, that you present your bodies." Now notice very carefully what follows. It is a little phrase which does not startle us because we know it so well. It certainly would have startled any Jew who read it, and it certainly would have startled any Gentile who read it at that time. I refer to the phrase, "a living sacrifice." That was something entirely new to the Jew, and entirely new to the Gentile; new to the Jew in the midst of all the ceremonial law of Hebraism; new to the Gentile amid all the sacrifices of his temple. A living sacrifice! Sacrifices were dead, and only became sacrifices when they were dead. Paul said, No, your body is to be presented a living sacrifice — not dead, not even mutilated. Paul was not calling Christians to an ascetic life, but exactly the reverse. Paul was not suggesting that we should strengthen our spiritual life by the mutilation of our bodies. That method is sensual and not spiritual, and the result it produces in the spirit is a sensual result, and not a high and holy result. The final condemnation of the false method is found in the records of the life of Jesus of Nazareth. He never flagellated Himself. His enemies did. He imposed upon Himself no restrictions that dwarfed and spoiled the natural forces of his body. Our bodies are to be presented a living sacrifice — not dead and not mutilated, but alive, and the more alive the better, the stronger the better. We are not asked to lay a carcase upon the altar. We are called to present a living man, that walks and runs and sings and laughs and works and realizes the fulness of the full measure of his humanity. Continuing, the Apostle adds to living the word "holy", that is, healthy.

Holy, that is, sanctified, healthy, in that it is separated to divine service, an instrument of the redeemed and ransomed spirit. The body healthy. Again there follows an arresting phrase — "well pleasing to God." That is an anti-Christian attitude that abuses the body, and speaks of it as being unworthy. The old Hebrew singer knew better when he said we are fearfully and wonderfully made. The body is God's creation. There is no mechanism like it. What strides we have made in mechanical science in the last fifty years; but we have never made a piece of machinery equal to the body in which we walk and move and express our spiritual nature, whether good or ill. The body is God's creation. Said that same singer: He knew my members when they did not exist. When I was curiously and wondrously wrought in the underparts of the world, God was the Maker; and up out of the mystery of the abyss He has brought the marvellous mystery of the body. A body is created for glorious activities, and in proportion as it is fulfilling its true functions, it is well pleasing to God. That ought not to be a surprising thing. It is not a surprising thing if we really believe in God and the God of the Bible. Everything is well pleasing to God, which He has made. "And He saw everything that He had made, and it was very good." And what had He made? Nature, the animals, the birds, the trees and supremely Man.

The birds, their wings and their songs; the cattle upon a thousand hills; the landscape at eventide when lowing cattle wend their way homeward. God is charmed with it all, and the proportion in which you are not is the proportion in which you do not know God. If this is true about cattle, what about men? God so loves to see the bairns at play that He says that when His city is built they shall play in the streets of it. Of course, they cannot do that in London because it is not His city yet. That is the meaning of the appeal concerning the body. No hard, harsh requirements, no cruel instruments of torture that abuse the flesh; but a spirit mastered by love, and a life mastered by a spirit that is mastered by God alone. Living sacrifices! Paul says that is worship, that is spiritual worship. All that is only possible as the spirit in its inner shrine and sanctuary yields itself up to the renewing of the mind, and walks in the light.

There are two inclusive ideas in this text. First as to reasonable service. That is the idea of personality fulfilling its highest function. The other is the proving of the will of God. That is the idea of personality realizing its deepest experience.

There is one inclusive argument in the text: by the compassions of God. If we need to be persuaded to this holy and full life we must get back to Calvary. By that Cross of bruising and spoiling, and all its mystic mystery, and that only, we can hope to live.

The final responsibility of my spirit, justified and no longer under condemnation, is to yield itself up to the life of the renewed mind and to take the body and make it express the fact in worship and service:

> Take my hands, and let them move
> At the impulse of Thy love.
> Take my feet, and let them be
> Swift and beautiful for Thee.
> Take my voice, and let me sing
> Ever, only for my King.

THE CALL OF CHRIST

Matthew 11:28.

"Come unto Me."

We are told in this historic narrative that Jesus uttered these words in the days of His flesh. He is still uttering the same call. For all the things that He said He says. His words were not words for a day or for an age but for every day and for all the ages, until humanity shall have found release and rest in the Divine Will.

But how may it be said that this is the call of Christ to-day? During the war I had been addressing a company of our boys in one of the huts, and on my way back to the place where I was staying I was joined by a young officer. He said to me: "Padre, may I walk with you?" Of course I said, "Certainly." He said, "May I talk to you?" and I said, "Certainly." He said, "May I say to you exactly what I am thinking?" I said, "That is what I would like to hear." "Well," he said "Padre, I am flippant"; and he was not; the next day he was going up the line, and men do not talk flippantly in those circumstances. He said, "You have been telling us in that hut to-night that Christ is calling us. I wish you would tell me what you mean." I was a little surprised, a little non-plussed; for we are very apt in the Christian Church to take for granted that the ordinary man understands our language, and sometimes he does not. I said to the young officer, "Tell me what you mean." He said, "I mean this. I believe in the story of Jesus, I am not an unbeliever,

THE CALL OF CHRIST

but I have heard parsons tell me all my life that Christ is calling me, and I have never heard Him call me. I believe He said the words He is recorded to have said, but when you tell us boys that Christ is calling us, I can only say honestly I never heard Him." I looked into his eyes and said, "Oh, yes, you have heard Him." He said, "I think not." "Well," I said, "come in and let us have a yarn." It was ten o'clock at night, and he left me at four in the morning.

The result of those hours with that fine fellow — he was an Oxford graduate and was talking with perfect honesty — led me to ask my question a moment ago: What do we mean when we say Christ is calling? If you were as honest as that young officer you might say exactly what he said, "We never heard Him." You have never heard a voice articulate in human accents calling you. Ah, but He is calling, calling, and calling all the time.

SUGGESTIONS FROM WITHOUT

We live in a strange world, the final facts of which we have not discovered. I do not mean this little planet; we know nearly all about that now, not quite. We live in a larger world than this, and there are spiritual forces playing round about us, beating in upon us all the time, making their impressions upon us, their appeals to us. For the moment I am not careful whether you think of those spiritual forces as personalities or not. Yet I remember no real appeal can ever be made to personalities except through personalities. When you find suddenly borne in upon your consciousness a suggestion that you sin, or that you do not sin, those suggestions do not emanate from your own personality, however deep and experienced it is. Always they come to you from without. You acknowledge this in your common speech when you say, "Suddenly there came a thought to me." Whence came it? Oh, the mystery of our human life and the largeness of the world in which we are living! How ignorant we are of it. Yet we know that suddenly, apparently out of the nowhere or out of the everywhere into the here, certain suggestions were made to us. We did not formulate the suggestion within our own personality; it came beating in upon us.

Depend upon it, the spiritual world round about us is influencing us all the time — more or less, and it is in that spiritual world that Christ is operative to-day. He who for a season was contracted to a span, as Wesley said, in the Incarnation, and then passed from human sight, was not dissipated into thin air; for the Man of Nazareth still lives at the right hand of God. Then there came a new movement in the world, the coming of the Holy Spirit, through Whom Christ is forevermore seeking men, calling men. Other voices are speaking to them from the spirit world, but He is speaking constantly by the Holy Spirit, and His one call is always this: "Come unto Me." In that call all doctrine is implicated, all theology is involved, all the height and depth and length and breadth of the mystery of the person of Christ is included.

THREE NOTES IN THE CALL

He is still calling. How are we to know His call? It operates within the spiritual realm, and I am going to submit to you that in the call of Christ there are three notes, and we may know when He is calling. Whenever either of these notes makes an appeal to our personality, mind and heart and will, that is Christ calling us to Himself. In the Gospel narratives that lie behind and round about this central call, expressed in words so simple, "Come unto Me," you have all His teaching, all His revelation, all that He said concerning man, concerning God, concerning the interrelations between them, and I want, so far as I am able — inadequately I know; I hope not inaccurately — to gather up and express in these three notes the whole of the things that constitute the call of Christ.

The first note in the call of Christ to me is the call of holiness; the central note is the call to hope; and the ultimate note is the call to heroism. I submit that His is the one and only voice which through the far-flung mystery and majesty of the ministry of the Spirit, is calling men in this way — the only one is Christ Himself. He is calling men to holiness. Who else is doing that to-day? He is calling men to hope. Who else with any inspirational authority is bidding this world hope in an hour like this? He is calling men to heroism to-day. There are other voices calling men to certain kinds of heroism, but in the last analysis the spirit of the age is best expressed by a little card that I saw hanging on a 'bus the other day: "Safety First." I am not objecting to it on a 'bus; it is good to have it there and to hang it on your motor car, and obey it. It is a good beginning. But when you make that your philosophy of life, the finding of the path of least resistance, the securing of ease for yourself, you are a pagan blasphemer against God and the universe. Christ is not saying that to you. His call is to high heroism.

HOLINESS

1. Let us take these three notes in sequence. Christ's call is the call to holiness. May I approach that along a negative line? Whenever you receive an impression made upon your mind from without, that sug-

gests to you that sin is desirable or inevitable or permissible, that is not the voice of Christ. That goes without saying. Then why did I say it? In order that I may say another thing. You never heard a voice suggest those things to you but that at the same moment another voice was contradicting the suggestion. Then the suggestion came to you perhaps through some human lips, or apart from human lips, by some spiritual influence breaking in upon your life in the realm of the underworld of evil. When the suggestion came to you that sin was desirable, permissible in certain circumstances, inevitable, there was always a voice that said, "No; refuse the call of sin, and stand for purity, goodness, holiness." That was the voice of Christ by the Holy Spirit calling you to stand with Him for holiness. Is it not so, that whenever we have had the suggestion of evil we have had the suggestion of good at the same moment? If someone says the suggestion of evil comes to him without any backward appeal towards goodness, then God help him! That is not the common experience of humanity. We talk of temptation; it is a common phrase. A man says: I was tempted to do thus, or so; I was tempted to do this evil thing. I was drawn towards it. Why did not you do it? Perhaps you did it, but not immediately, there was hesitation; perhaps you did not do it. Why not? Whether ultimately you yielded or not, with the suggestion there was also a voice calling you to refuse, to be true, to be pure, to be good. God suffers not any man to be tempted above that he is able to bear, and with the temptation He always makes a way of escape, and the way of escape is flung up before the soul because there is always the appeal to holiness. That is the voice of Christ: "Come unto Me." — the Holy One, the spotless One, the sinless One, the One undefiled and separate from sin, Son of Man and Son of God. By the Holy Spirit, He is repeating the call of Purity to men everywhere, and the fundamental note in the call of Christ is that which calls men to holiness. Have you not heard that call? Have you not heard it all your lives? I do not mean through the lips of preachers now — through them also. I do not mean through the lips of Sabbath school teachers — through them also. I do not mean through the tender emotion of the appeal of father and mother — through them also. But all the while Someone calling, Someone halting me when I would have gone wrong, when I did wrong; the restraint upon my spirit, the call to holiness — that is Christ's call.

Christ never calls any man to mercy save that behind the call to mercy is the intention of righteousness. The moment in which we preach the Gospel of the Lord Jesus Christ as though it were a Divine provision by which men may dodge the consequences of their sin and continue in sin, we blaspheme against God and against the whole universe. Christ came in to the world to make men pure, holy, good, and His call is sounded ever in the ears of men; yes, through the preacher's word; yes, through the witness of the Church; but also in out-of-the-way places where no preacher's voice is heard, where the function of the teacher cannot be fulfilled, where men and women are in loneliness, Christ is calling; and the call to holiness persists like the ether through the universe, vibrating over the mountains and through the valleys, speaking to men, seeking the human soul everywhere. That is Christ calling, calling, calling — "Come unto Me."

HOPE

2. There is another note, and it is the central note in the call of Christ — the call to hope. If there were not this note in the call of Christ, if the call of Christ were only a call to holiness, I would quit preaching. Why? Because I myself am utterly unequal to obey that call unless He do something more for me than present an ideal and call me to fulfill it. I could not mock humanity by preaching to them the ethical call of Christ which I myself am entirely unable to fulfil unless I have something else — the note of hope. May I come to that also along the negative line for a moment? Whenever you hear a voice suggesting to you that your case is hopeless, morally and spiritually, that your past dereliction necessitates constant and ultimate dereliction; whenever you hear anyone, man or spirit, saying to you that you cannot be pure, that is never the voice of Christ. His voice is for ever contradicting the dark, sinister pessimism that declares to a man that he cannot be free from the power of sin, and cannot attain unto holiness. He comes not merely with the demand for holiness, but He comes with the note of hope.

Once more, take these Gospel narratives, and at your leisure go through them carefully and watch Jesus dealing with the individual. Miss out the things He said to multitudes, the great discourses and discussions, and watch Him whenever you see Him dealing with an individual. Among other things, this will impress you supremely, that when He came into the presence of the human soul He was the most unrepentant optimist that the world has ever known. You never find Him admitting that a case is hopeless. Men and women were saved, — or made whole — the terms

THE CALL OF CHRIST

are synonymous in the New Testament, sometimes down in the realm of the physical and often in the realm of the spiritual — by their faith in Him; and, not invariably, but constantly, you will discover that their faith in Him was created by His faith in them. When no one believed in a man, in a woman, Jesus did, and His belief in them created their belief in Him. He brought hope to those who were helpless.

Take the account of His first meeting with Simon. Andrew brought his brother to Jesus, and Jesus looking at him said: "Thou art Simon the son of Jona; thou shalt be called Rock." The significant thing in the story is that Simon did not answer. There were two things Simon Peter never did successfully; one was to sit still, the other was to shut his mouth. I think I am related to him! That day never a word passed his lips. Why? Because he had never been startled as he was when Jesus said he should be rock. It was the one thing he was not. Study that personality, study it psychologically in the Bible page — for the Bible is full of psychology — and you will find that here was a man who had all the elements of human strength within him. He was a man of tremendous intellectual capacity, of marvellous emotional power, of vast volitional strength; and yet he was one of the weakest of men. He was Peter Pan — the boy that never grew up. Barrie's quaint and delightful conceit is a lovely story for children and a rotten philosophy for a man; for any man who does not grow up is a failure. Simon had never grown up. He had all the elements of personality, but not welded together, not cohesive, not consistent, and to use a very forceful but inelegant Americanism, he was always slopping over. Jesus looked at him and said: Man, you shall be rock;

you have been the kind of man that nobody could depend on, that nobody could build on; you shall be rock, a man that other men can build on, welded into cohesion and consistency and strength. But believing in him when nobody else believed in him Jesus captured Peter, and hope sprang up within his soul. There is another illustration, perhaps more wonderful, taking too long for detailed consideration, but to which I would make hurried reference; you find it in John VIII:1-8. Christ is always bringing hope to the soul. Does that simple story of the woman taken in sin bring to you a wistful wonder whether after all you, too, can be recovered from leprosy and made pure and beautiful? That is Christ calling. Whenever the crushed soul moves out into a new realm of wistful hope, if it seems as though the flush of new morning is rising and the song of the birds is singing in your soul again, that is Christ calling: "Come unto Me," and that because He is able to take hold of a man of slack personality such as Simon was and make him a man, unified and strong as a rock, as Simon became; because He is able to take hold of a woman, broken, bruised, soiled, and make her a woman of refinement and beauty, satisfying all God's demands. He hopes for me because of what He is, He makes me hope because of what He is able to do, and His call is always a call to hope.

HEROISM

3. Christ's call is the call to heroism. Any voice that suggests to you that the best way through life is the easy way is the voice of hell. Any impression borne in upon your soul which suggests to you that what you need is the religion of ease and quietness is the voice of evil seducing and blinding you. Christ never suggested that to the souls of men; He never

told any man that it was easy to be a Christian, a disciple, a follower of Himself. He talked of cutting off the right hand, and plucking out the right eye, and forsaking father, mother, wife and children, and renouncing all one has and taking up a cross and following Him. He is always appealing to the heroic, always showing men that life is a serious thing, deadly serious because of sin, and that the only way of deliverance is that of submission to Him, and that the way of fellowship with Him is the Cross. He is calling you to high heroism. Other voices will offer you a good time, a pleasant way; not He. Oh, surely, yes, a good time, but the good time to come when life is seen in its bigness and in its heroic demands, and adventure through blood and fire and smoke, until the Kingdom come.

I think the Church of God has made a great mistake with its young people along that line. It was said to them too constantly, "Come with us, and we will do you good." I believe in my deepest soul that the appeal to high heroism is the appeal that will win and hold the youth of to-day. I think we insult young life when we simply say, we will do you good, give you a pleasant time. God forgive us! Christ is calling youth to holiness, to hope, to heroism, to sacrificial life and sacrificial service, to a splendid, magnificent adventure. Do you hear a voice calling you to yield your life up to holiness, to personal realization through redeeming grace, and all that you may go out into the broad highway of the world in healing and heroic ministry, lifting humanity by serving it? That is the voice of Christ calling.

How are we to obey, to answer the threefold call? Consent to His call to holiness, that is repentance;

consent to His call to hope, that is faith; consent to His call to heroism, that is surrender and consecration. "Come unto Me." Where is He? Just where you are — "Closer is He than breathing, nearer than hands or feet." In that sacred and wonderful shrine of your own inner personality, that I cannot invade, thank God, that I have no right to invade, in the loneliness of your own spirit say, "O Christ, I am Thine!" And in that act you will find the secret of holiness, the joy of hope, and the beginning of high and heroic life.

The only preparation for the morrow is the right use of today. The morrow comes for naught, if today is not needed. — Bowen.

God takes men's hearty desires and will, instead of the deed, when they have not power to fulfil it; but He never took the bare deed instead of the will. — Richard Baxter.

THE COMING GLORY

Titus 2:11-13.

"For the grace of God hath appeared, bringing salvation to all men, instructing us, to the intent that, denying ungodliness and worldly lusts, we should live soberly and righteously and godly in this present world, looking for the blessed hope and appearing of the glory of our God and Saviour, Jesus Christ."

Men are universally conscious of incompleteness, incompleteness in the realization of individual ideals, incompleteness in the realization of a social order, incompleteness in national and international affairs, incompleteness in the race itself.

It is not only such as are members of the Church of Jesus Christ who are conscious of this. It is a part of the common consciousness of enlightened humanity — one of the co-incident experiences of advancement is this assurance of imperfection. In every age and in every clime men have looked forward to some better order of things. If they have not always so expressed it, men everywhere have lived in the belief that there is, after all,

> One far-off Divine event
> To which the whole creation moves.

No man is really ever satisfied with his own position, with his own times. If we could be silent enough, and if our hearing were acute enough, we should hear the whole race ever sighing and sobbing for something better.

The Christian fact has not brought that consciousness to the race, but it has come to interpret it — to fulfil it — and the proportion in which we are Christian men and women is the proportion in which the sigh has become a song, the hope has become a prophecy, the wonder has become a certainty, the mist has become a glory.

Our subject now is what the Christian faith says with regard to that hope of the race. I shall speak first of the place of hope in the economy of grace; secondly, of the nature of the hope which grace presents; and finally of the particular application of the hope to the life of the child of God.

GRACE AND GLORY

First, then, the place of hope in the economy of grace. Grace is the necessary prelude to glory. Paul, in writing to the Romans, made an all-inclusive charge against humanity. "All have sinned and fall short of the glory of God." The highest note in the anthem he sings concerning the work of Jesus is "We rejoice in hope of the glory of God." Between that statement of failure and that statement of hope lies the unveiling of the great plan of salvation — the gospel of the grace of God. Grace brings salvation, chastises men into perfection of life, exerts through such lives the influence that denies ungodliness and worldly lusts, and so paves the way for the march of glory, prepares the hour for its outshining.

It is not merely true that grace is the necessary prelude to glory. It is equally true that glory is the necessary sequel to grace. Let men be saved, let character be re-created, let the race be redeemed, let every individual live the life sober, righteous, godly — then what? Then glory must follow not as something which is the crowning of grace, but as something which is the outworking of grace.

GRACE FOR GRACE

In the great gospel of the mystery of the Son of God, I read: "For of His fulness we are received, and grace for grace"; and in Paul's letter to the Corinthians, "But we all, with unveiled face reflecting as a mirror the glory of the Lord, are transformed into the same image from glory to glory, even as from the Lord the Spirit."

John says we received His grace, grace for grace. That is, every line of beauty that was manifest in Jesus is to be realized in us. Have you seen the grace of His compassion? You shall have the grace of His compassion and be compassionate. Have you seen the grace of His lowliness? You shall have the grace of His lowliness and be lowly. Have you seen the grace of His power? You shall have the grace of His power and be powerful.

But what is the issue? Granted the grace of the Son of God, realized in human character, what is the issue? The glory of the Son of God is realized in human character, so that Paul says, not grace for grace, but "from glory unto glory," being transformed into his perfect likeness.

The epiphany of glory will be a definite event. That to which the apostle refers in my test is not merely the glory that is seen to-day but something that is not yet seen — a finality, an issue, a consummation — something yet far on, and out of sight. Our Lord expected that it would be definite and personal, and that its definiteness and its personality were alike homed within Himself. Our Lord said: "If any man shall be ashamed of Me and of My words, of him shall the Son of Man be ashamed." When? "When He cometh in His own glory, and the glory of the Father, and of the holy angels." You cannot construe the words of Jesus to mean any spiritual coming, as something different from and contradictory to the fact of a personal advent.

HEAVEN ON EARTH

But do not let us think of the second advent of Jesus in any small way. The first advent began nineteen centuries ago, and all this is still part of it. The second advent must have its beginning, but be very careful how you put measurement upon its issue. He will come to gather His own to Himself, to set up the true order on the earth, to bring in the Golden Age. People are singing about heaven, thinking about heaven, and writing letters about heaven, and even writing books about heaven. There is nothing wrong in all that, providing they have not a wrong idea of what heaven is. They go to Revelation, and read the story of the wonderful city, and they think it is heaven. It is not heaven. The city that John saw in Patmos is not heaven. Heaven will never come out of heaven. That city comes out of heaven, and is established here on the earth. The nations of the world are to walk in the light of that city. The picture is not a picture of the heaven to which we go. It is a picture of how God at last will set us His Kingdom here upon the earth. It is not a picture of how we shall win heaven. It is the picture of how God will win earth. And all this is connected with the second advent of Jesus.

The issues of sin are sorrow, disease, poverty, and all crime. When He comes the second time He will come to banish sorrow, to banish disease, to make poverty impossible, to hold crime in absolute check among the sons of men. When He comes again He will rule with a rod of iron. Have you read that passage and trembled at it? Have you ever dared to quote it to show that He will be arbitrary and unkind? The rod of iron. What is it? The rod of iron is the rod of perfect straightness and unswerving equity. There is nothing the world needs today so much as justice that can neither be bought nor sold. Justice that will be as easily meted out to the man who cannot afford it as to the man who can. Yes, we are crying for mercy; we need it. God have mercy upon us! But we need justice, too, as between man and man. Have you ever thought of one of the old prophetic words about His rule? "He shall not judge after the seeing of his eyes or by the hearing of his ears." The only way in which we can judge today is by the seeing of the eye and hearing of the ear. No man was committed to prison yesterday for long or short period, but by judgment that depended upon the seeing of the eyes and hearing of the ears. I am not criticizing it. We cannot do any better. But He will do better.

When He comes and begins His great and gracious reign all the things that issue from sin will be banished — poverty, disease and sorrow, and all else.

THE DREAM OF THE RACE

But the first advent was not merely the bringing of redemption; it was also for regeneration. Follow it to its issue. The regeneration of the individual must issue in the true communion, communism, social order. The end of self means the end of strife. When each man thinks not only on his own things, but also on the things of others, we shall have the true social order. When every man knows God to be his Father and lives in right relation, the dream of the race will be realized. The restoration of individuals to communion with God must issue in the restoration of society to communion with God. What is that but the establishment of the Theocracy, the direct government of men by God?

I do not believe in democracy. I believe that democracy would be a far viler despotism that any the world has ever seen. I believe in an absolute monarchy, providing you find the true monarch. God has found Him, and the world has not received Him. But the true order is one supreme and only King, God; and all men living in obedience to His government and in mutual inter-relationship.

All this does not interfere with the question of whether He comes secretly or not. I am speaking of the whole fact of the second advent, in all its stages, parts, and issues, and these greater and larger truths of the glory of God.

WHAT IS GOD'S GLORY?

What is the glory of God? God is glorified in the realization of the purpose of His own heart. The flower that blossoms perfectly glorifies God because it is what God meant it to be. The sun that shines in midday glorifies God because it is what God meant it to be. A man glorifies God when he is what God meant him to be. God will be glorified in human history when men have found His law, yielded to it, realized in their own persons and society all that God meant them to be. God's glory is not something with which he decorates himself as men decorate themselves in trappings. God's glory is the realization in the whole of His creation of the high purpose of His heart. And Christian faith sings the song of the coming glory. In the Pauline anthem, when He tells us we were justified by faith, that we have peace with God, that we have access by grace into the favour wherein we stand, he closes with the words: "And rejoice in hope of the glory of God."

How we have spoiled that passage by imaging that the apostle meant that He saves us, and bids us hope for heaven. That is not rejoicing in hope of the glory of God. You, young man, young maiden, with the bloom of health upon your cheek and the elasticity of youth in your very step; do you imagine that you "rejoice in hope of the glory of God" when you hope to reach heaven? That is not what the apostle meant. What he meant was this: "We rejoice in hope" that at last God will be glorified, not by our reaching heaven, but by His possessing earth. The glory of God, in hope of which we rejoice, is the establishment of the Divine order upon the earth, and grace is working toward that end.

The second advent will be a crisis that will gather up the work we have been doing and lead it on to future issues. Nothing is lost. What you have said to your Sunday-school class is not lost. The message you delivered in the open air is not lost. The prayers you are praying, mother, are not lost. Nothing is lost that is done in grace and compassion. You are flinging into human history forces that will wait for a crisis, and when, presently, the crisis comes, then prayers long uttered and forgotten will be answered; seeds flung into barren soil which have seemed to be dead will bloom into beauty. Glory will be the realization of all that grace meant; and when the King comes next it is to wind everything up and finish — it is to begin the administration and set up the order on the earth.

THE NEW EARTH

And dear old earth! Let no man abuse the earth.

If you have any abuse, heap it on your own head. We have not begun to realize all its secrets. Dear old mother earth will laugh with flowers when the King reigns. O for His reign of perfect equity, of judgment! "Lord, come quickly," is the cry of the people who feel the pain and pang of earth's unutterable sorrow. This is the hope of the glory of God, the certainty that presently He will come and take into His own service the things that are being discovered, and used, alas! today too often in wrong ways. Presently He will come and put His pierced hand upon the whole, and use them for carrying out the purposes of God and establishing upon the poor, bruised earth the breadth, beauty and beneficence of the Divine Kingdom.

I am not at all anxious about getting to heaven. God will take care of that. I shall see Him and reach that home by and by; but oh! I am anxious about earth.

APPLICATION TO THE BELIEVER

My concluding word concerns the particular application of this advent to the believer. Here I come at once into a narrow sphere. I only come that I may speak a word of comfort and helpfulness to the child of God. What application has that advent to the believer personally? First of all, it is the perpetual light that makes the present bearable. I pause because so many Christians today do not seem to live in the light of it. I sometimes wonder how they bear the toil, how they endure the suffering! I never lay my head upon the pillow without thinking it may be that before morning break, the last morning will break, and the King will come. I declare quietly and solemnly, that if you take that away from me, and tell me I have to convert the world by the preaching of the Gospel, then I give the whole thing up. But tell me I have to evangelize the world, to proclaim the news, and that presently He will come and consumate the work; then I sing at my work, and wait for the moving that presages the dawn, and long for the breaking of the light. That is the chief value, I think, of the advent in the personal life of the believer.

REUNION

It will also mean reunion with the loved ones gone before. Do not be sorrowful as though you had no hope. Do not be anxious about those fallen on asleep. "If we believe that Jesus died and rose again, even so them also which sleep in Jesus will God bring with Him." The first advent compels the second, and it is the first advent which is the rock upon which my faith fastens and sings the song of the coming victory. You ask me how? You tell me you do not see the way? I tell you grace has been manifested, and though I cannot see all the method I am certain of the issue.

> How do the rivulets find their way?
> How do the flowers know the day,
> And open their cups to catch the ray?
>
> I see the germ to the sunlight reach,
> And the nestling know the old bird's speech;
> I do not see who is there to teach.
>
> I see the hare from the danger hide,
> And the star through the pathless spaces ride;
> I do not see that they have a guide.
>
> He is eyes for all who is eyes for the mole,
> All motion goes to the rightful goal;
> Oh, God! I can trust for the human soul!

"JACOB'S WRESTLING"

Genesis 32:24.

"And Jacob was left alone; and there wrestled a man with him until the breaking of the day."

Twenty years have passed away, or thereabouts, since the night of vision and of blessing of which we spoke together last Sabbath e'en. Jacob has had strange and perplexing experiences in the intervening years. He reached the land that he set out to seek; he met Laban, and for these long and weary years, as they must have been, he has been having personal and daily contact with Laban. And if there be any satisfaction to be gathered out of the keen, shrewd capacity for business that Jacob evidenced, it is that one is thankful that such a man had to do with Laban. For of all the men profoundly mean whose lives are mentioned in the Book of God, Laban is easily first, and I think Jacob came out of it very well, and my gratitude is always great that Laban found his match when Jacob went to stay with him. That may be a carnal sort of gratitude — you will forgive and forget it as I go on. But Laban is just one of those sort of men whose successors are in the world today, who will use anyone who believes in God for his own ends; the kind of men who like to have a godly man as his cashier because he knows it is safe, but he himself may be as ungodly as you please; the kind of man who will trade with Christianity because there is in it the element that makes for his own aggrandizement, and then will fling it away like the rind of an orange he has done with. That was Laban. He will get everything out of Jacob's confidence in God he can, and he will trick him and cheat him every chance he gets. Those must have been very trying years for Jacob. I believe if you could have looked at Jacob just where we meet him here in this part of Genesis you would have seen a man of remarkable aspect and bearing, hard, keen, alert, and yet with the lines on his face that tell of an embittered soul; for no man ever passes through such a period of business transactions as those twenty years in the life of Jacob without having become in some sense hardened in the process, distrustful of his fellow-men. And as I look at Jacob on that night when, marvellously manipulating all the circumstances of the moment, he prepares for what lies ahead, and then goes down to loneliness and God, I think you will have seen a man erect, though old, having upon him all the marks of a sinuous strength, and all the tokens of an embittered spirit.

But this is a remarkable day for Jacob. He called the place "Mahanaim," that is, the place of hosts. Jacob is in the midst of strange companies. Laban has kissed him and gone home. A pity he did not go without kissing him. It is another touch in Laban's character. And the hosts of Laban have departed. And then a strange thing happened, as men count things strange — a host of angels passed across the plain. I do not know whether anybody saw them but Jacob, but he saw them. Laban's hosts have gone, and then God's hosts. Do you think at that moment memories came thronging back of the marvelous vision twenty years before — the ladder, angels, Jehovah? This host of God simply swept across his vision and passed out of sight, and then the attention of the man is turned to another host. "Jacob sent messengers before him to Esau, his brother, unto the land of Seir," and Jacob said to these messengers, "Go and tell Esau that his servant Jacob, who has been sojourning with Laban, and stayed until now" — and I always think there is a peculiarly sorrowful and cynical emphasis in that "And stayed until now," as much as to say, "Oh, if Esau knew what Laban was he would congratulate me upon having stayed so long and getting away at last." — "and I have oxen, and asses and flocks, and menservants and maidservants; and I have sent to tell my lord that I may find grace in thy sight. And the messengers returned to Jacob, saying, "We came to thy brother Esau, and moreover he cometh to meet thee, and four hundred men with him." Another host! It was a day of hosts! Laban's hosts had departed; God's hosts had swept across the vista of his vision; and Esau's host is coming to meet him with armed men.

JACOB'S RECONCILIATION WITH ESAU.

Now look carefully for a moment at the man before we follow him over the Jabbok to the night of wrestling. And I beg you to mark all Jacob's characteristics coming out in this wonderful scene. He did not first send a present to Esau; he first sent messengers to say he was coming, and if the answer which the messengers bring had been a peaceful answer — and I hope I do not do Jacob an injustice when I say it — I do not think he would ever have offered Esau a present. What brings this man back? Old times, old associations. Anything else? surely yes — the covenant of God, the blessing promised. Do you remember the words of Jehovah to him in that night of vision twenty years before? "I am the God of Abraham, and the God of Isaac . . . And lo, I am with thee, and will keep thee, and will bring thee again into this land." That is in the heart of Jacob, and he has come back into the land. To possess the land is his ambition, to possess the land he knows to be God's purpose for him, so that so far God's purpose and Jacob's ambition move along the same lines. God wills that Jacob should possess this land. Jacob desires supremely to possess the land of his father and of his father's father, and for that purpose he is coming home. And the first thing to do is to find out what condition of mind Esau is in — he sent his messenger. There comes back the answer that I have already referred to; "Esau is coming to meet thee, not in peace, but in anger, armed, bringing 400 men with him." And then it is that all the diplomacy and the policy of the man appears. He must now placate Esau; he must now win the favour of his brother; he must now overcome the prejudices of his brother, he must do something to blot out from his brother's mind the memory of his own past incredible meanness, and he will divide himself into three bands, and he will send presents by the first as though that were all; and in case they are not enough the second band will come with the second installment of the present; and in case the second fails the third shall move on. Mark the policy of the man. If there had been no warlike approach on the part of Esau — no present; if the first installment of the present had pacified him the second would have been kept back; if the second had done that which the first had failed to do the third would not have been offered. You are quite sure you understand his policy. Many of you would have done the same, it is human nature; it is the ordinary commercial spirit at its best. I am not saying there is anything wrong about it; I only want you to see the man. And then there is a tender touch, for every rough and rugged man has a tender spot somewhere, and the man most shrivelled and embittered with life has got some inner chamber of his heart in which there is a sweet and gracious aroma of gentleness, if you could only find it, and I like this last thing — he takes over his wives, Leah and Rachel, and all the children, and guards them carefully, and then he goes back across that little stream, the Jabbok, babbling on its way and making strange music even in the night hours, and he was left alone. And now we come to the point of particular observation. "There wrestled a man with him until the breaking of the day." Let us, so far as it is possible, observe the wrestling of that long night and deduce from it certain lessons of perpetual application.

JACOB ALONE AT JABBOK

Now, first of all, we must look at the man Jacob when he was left alone. There are three things to be said about him; he was successful; he was straightened; he was self-confident. Successful. We read these stories sometimes and hardly notice them; I mean the phrasing of them does not express to us at first sight all that it ought to do. He said to his brother Esau; "With my staff I passed over this Jordan," he said it to God, too, in prayer — "and now I am become two bands." The expression "two bands" is a very small one in your hearing and in mine, but it means "great wealth." Twenty years ago he had left home, not a young man by any means. I have known sermons preached about that first journey to young men. Very well, he was seventy years old, and never forget it, and if you stay at home until you are seventy years you will be doing pretty well. At seventy years of age he had left home, and when he left home he had carried nothing with him but a staff, the symbol of his calling; and after these twenty years of bargaining and dealing with Laban he is coming back with two bands, all the wealth that he has gathered with him; and wealth then in Eastern countries, as it is still, was represented by the cattle and the flocks; two bands — a wealthy man. And yet, look closely at him, and you will find that this man is not satisfied. Why not? The past is recurring, the things that he left behind when he carried his staff over Jordan, are coming back to him; those very things of which we spoke last Sabbath evening — the meanness by which he robbed his brother of his birthright, the trickery by which he obtained the outward expression of blessing from his father. These things are rising before him. He wants to get back to the home land, to the old familiar fields and plains, to the speech which is as music in his ear, as the dialect of your home country is always musical when you have wandered far away. He wants to get back to this land which has been given to his father and to his grandfather, and promised to him, but dwelling in the land are the results of his wrong-doing in that land twenty years before. And the man successful is the man straightened; he is not satisfied; his getting has brought him no real, deep peace of heart and conscience, for while, it may be, tending the flocks of his father-in-law, and making his own two bands, he had forgotten or driven back out of memory the wrong of past days; but traveling now that long journey from the North country down to the South, coming again over the river and into the old familiar places, the old wrong springs up and he knows in his heart of hearts that the sin of the past, the wrong of the past, is not yet atoned. And yet, as I look at him again in his loneliness, before the hand Divine is laid upon him, I see not merely a successful man and a straightened man, but a self-confident man. Here is a man believing in God, believing in the purpose of God, and firmly convinced that he will win his way into the realization of a Divine purpose by his own personal planning and personal effort, and, as we have already seen, his policy with Esau marks the self-confident man. And now I watch him at his prayer, I listen to his prayer, and I cannot read that prayer carefully and watch God's dealings with the man without coming to feel that his very prayers are part of his own policy for winning his own battle and accomplishing his own end. How many men there are that pray this way? I do not deny the sincerity of their prayer. I do not deny they believe in God as they pray. The very prayer of such men is proof of their belief in God. Jacob was too keen, too shrewd, too material, too matter-of-fact to pray if he had not believed that within prayer there lay a power that tended toward victory; but it was his prayer that helped him to win; it was by his policy and then his intercession that he would win his way back to the land and back into blessing. And, my brothers and sisters, it is just in that way that I want you to see him. I pause for a moment on the first point, for everything depends on our right understanding of his position. A man profoundly believing in the God of his father and of his grandfather, profoundly believing that from that night twenty years

"JACOB'S WRESTLING" 71

ago when he discovered God where he had least thought to find Him, God had been with him, a man really believing in Divine purpose, really believing that God meant to bring him into blessing; and yet a man by no means at the end of himself, but a man perfectly self-confident who will make his plan and his programme, who will pursue his own policy, and then to finish what he himself begins will lay hands upon prayer and compel God to help him to win his victory.

JACOB'S VICTORY — AND GOD'S

Now, having looked at the man for a moment, I pray you make the struggle. "There wrestled a man with him." We do wrong when we say that Jacob wrestled with the man. Of course, in a sense it is true, but let us abide by scriptural phraseology and scriptural declaration if we are dealing with scriptural subjects — "And there wrestled a man with him." It was not that there came to Jacob that night an angel visitor, and Jacob, seeing his opportunity, took hold of him and overpowered him. That is not the story. It was not that Jacob gained a victory by persistance over an angel; it was rather that the man — the angel man, the angel of the covenant taking human form in that night of wrestling — put his hand upon Jacob and wrestled with him till he won, till God won. Jacob won his victory certainly; he won his victory because God won His, and Jacob passed into the larger life and the larger victory through that night, because in it he, the self-confident man was defeated, broken, crippled, and then in weakness and tears and in supplication cast himself back upon God. And the one thing that wins victories with God is human weakness abandoning itself to Divine strength. "There wrestled a man with him." And who is this strange man, the possessor of the man stripped to Jacob's level? For, remember, the Incarnation was not the first theophany; God had again and again Himself in varied forms appeared to the sons of men in the past, sometimes as an angel. He appeared here, not as an angel even, but as a man, a strange man. God stripped to the level of Jacob, taking hold upon Jacob in such a way as to make Jacob exert at the utmost that strength in which he is confident in order that it may be broken, in order that through the defeat the dawn of victory, through the end of self-satisfaction may come the erect victory of a man that henceforth is in comradeship with God. "There wrestled a man with him."

Watch Jacob for a moment or two through these hours — still opposing, feeling upon him the touch of a man, hardly conscious, as I venture to think, at the beginning that behind the human touch there was the Divine, for remember, after the victory was won he looked into the face of a man and said to him, "Tell me thy name, I pray thee," feeling that here was some strange and unexpected visitor suddenly presenting himself with that night over the Jabbok, perchance one of the hosts that he had seen pass by him that day, and yet a man, a strange visitor — no accounting for him. And yet Jacob felt that as that hand was put upon him, now was the opportunity to win a victory, and as the man wrestled with Jacob toward the point of Jacob's defeat, Jacob resisted, fought, endeavored to win victory through strength, and so the hours of the night passed on. And the strength of Jacob's self-confidence is discovered in the fact that not until the light of a coming day was flushing the mountain yonder did he give in, and then the man that wrestled with him said to him, "Let me go, for the day breaketh." And then what? Now, my brothers, my sisters, there is so much in tone and in emphasis we often say, and I am more and more convinced of it as I read my Bible. What did he say? Did he say: "I will not let thee go except thou bless me"? No, he said nothing of the kind; and it was because he did not say that—and so many people think he did say that—that I read that little verse in the Prophet of Hosea, which is an illumination of that scene for us: "Yes, he had power over the angel and prevailed." But how? "He wept, and made supplication unto him." It is not the voice of strenuous self-assertion that wins with God: it is the broken, pleading voice of a man that is beaten. For God has touched him to the point of crippling; the hand of the man has now been put upon him in such a way that his thigh is strained, and in that moment when his strength is fast ebbing away and he finds he is mastered in the realm of physical life, then, with tears and entreaties and a sob of defeat he flings himself upon the man that wrestles with him and says in words and tones choked with emotion; "I will not let thee go except thou bless me", and that weeping man has won the victory, that suppliant soul, clinging to Omnipotence, when wounded, has won the victory. But God has won the victory; God has brought this man to the point of conscious defeat. For once Jacob is beaten; he tricked Esau and Isaac, he has outwitted Laban, but for once a hand has been upon him stronger than men, and Jacob has discovered, in the long, lone hours of the night, that some one he does not know perfectly yet— he will presently—is stronger than he; and in the moment when he sobs his surrender he wins his victory. And then, in great and condescending grace, the God who wins the fight tells him that he has won — "Thou hast prevailed. What is thy name?" What a confession! Jacob — supplanter — the one who has no right to anything. Priority of birth, and birthright, and of blessing, all wrong — supplanter. One wonders how this man had loved his name at all during those years; Jacob — "supplanter." And then came the answer: "Thou shalt be called no more 'Jacob,' but 'Israel' " literally, very literally — "wrestler with God" — by use and custom and intention. "Prince," for as a prince hast thou power with God and with men." With men he had won his victory by the strength of his nature; with God he had won his victory by yielding to the superior force and finding out at last his Master.

'ISRAEL FOR JACOB'

At last the man leaves Jacob, and Jacob takes his way back over the Jabbok. And I imagine that I go to the little company of people who are waiting for him, people who little know what has been passing over yonder, and I see him coming. There he comes. "What is the matter with him; he is positively limping. Last night when he left us and went down over the river he was quite erect, though a man of ninety years, walking with all the strength and sinewy strength of a young man, but this morning he comes back limping!" And as he comes I go and meet him, and I say: "What . . . . . ," "No, no," he says, "do not call me Jacob." "Surely, what is the matter that your name is no more?" "Israel, is my name; a supplanter no longer, but a prince." "Jacob, hast thou been dreaming?" "No, I have been wide awake." What makes thee limp?" And he would have told you had you asked him: "That halting upon my thigh is my paten of nobility. I walked erect last night a supplanter; I limp this morning a prince, and through the days that remain to me, be they many or few, the mark of my breaking is the brand of my making. I found some one last night stronger than I am. I outwitted Esau; I was one too many for my old father, Isaac; I have got all these bands from Laban; but last night a hand came upon me that was very human in its touch and I laid hold again to gain another advantage, but I did not get one single inch of headway through the hours, until at last I was crippled and beaten, and then with sobs and tears I flung myself on the wrestler in the darkness, and he changed my name and my nature. And I would rather have this limp with the experience of the night than walk erect through all my days a supplanter merely.

THE CROWN RIGHTS OF JEHOVAH

My brothers and sisters, I have dwelt longer than perhaps I intended upon the narrative itself, but I feel truth bears upon its wings lessons for us. And in all brevity let me in conclusion name and enforce one or two of them. What is the supreme lesson one learns when he reads that narrative carefully? It is this: a lesson concerning the crown rights of Jehovah. That is the first. There are many others, but that is the first. He possesses the land; not Esau dwelling in it, not Jacob journeying toward it; and if a man will possess the land he must receive it from God, no other man ever can possess. The goal at which you aim and at which I am in life, if it be a rightful goal — and I dismiss from the argument all the goals that are wrong because this goal was a right one; it was God's intention for the man — the goal which you aim at in life, which you are sure is God's plan for you, how will you reach it? Only as God opens the door. Now here is the subtle mistake of all spiritual life, as I venture to think. I am not speaking to the man who has chosen his own way; I am not talking to the man who has planned his own life without belief in God. There is a man here who believes in God, and that man knows in his heart of hearts what God's purpose in the world is for him. Some great capacities bestowed which marks the line of your life, about which there is no doubt, but have you learned this lesson — the land which you possess when God gives it to you. It is the deepest lesson of all human life — the crowned right of Jehovah, He bestows the blessing. So many things that we want are in His will for us, and we endeavor to obtain them, but we shall never obtain them so; what God wants me to have I must take from God; it is not enough that I know He wishes me to have it, and then endeavor to get it — this is wrong, the philosophy of life underlying it is false, and sooner or later must work ruin. And if a man runs toward a divinely-marked goal without recognition of God, if a man attempts to realize for himself what God has determined for him, that man is living the Jacob life, and sooner or later God will meet him on the way and teach him that these things must be received immediately from Him. And supposing it were possible for me to find my way into some land of promise that God has called me to without God — what then? It would be a sorry business. Past mistakes will meet Jacob coming back into the land without God, and spoil the very

God-given possession; the present difficulties will overwhelm him, and it is in infinite love that God checks him on his entrance to the land, and teaches him this hard, centre, initial, first lesson of all high life, that what God wills for me God must get for me and give to me. And I have no true possession save by coming to Him with empty hands and saying; "Thou art the Father of Lights; from Thee cometh the good and the perfect gift".

THE FOLLY OF SELF-CONFIDENCE

And then, brothers, necessarily, if the first lesson of the story is that of the crown rights of Jesus, the next by sequence and necessity is that of the folly of self-confidence. It is very easy to say it, it is not as easy to learn it. I speak tonight, I am perfectly sure, in the hearing of a great many people who have learned the lesson. I speak in the hearing of a great many who have not learned it. My dear brother, you may outwit a Laban, you may even manage by your diplomacy to conciliate an Esau, but you have not finished, there is another authority, and your dissatisfied heart, with the outwitting of Laban and the conciliating of Esau, proves that you have not yet found the deepest, truest rest. Supposing Jacob had fought his own way into the land, and having outwitted Laban had also conciliated Esau and had set right by diplomacy all the mistakes of the past, what would have been the result in the character of Jacob? Self-satisfaction. And that is why God cripples you and breaks you, to bring you into His will alone, because even if you won your way into the land of spiritual achievement by yourself you would come to be more self-satisfied in spiritual achievement than you were before, and spiritual pride will be a worse fall and ruin than any other form of pride that has cursed your life. Man must depend on God, and God in grace will meet men on the threshold of their greatest victory and shut the door and take them to some long, lone night of wrestling, until He brings them to the point of defeat that is for evermore the point of a great victory.

CHRIST'S PERPETUAL DEPENDENCE ON GOD

In conclusion let me say — and I know you will at once observe the application to my subject of what I now say — Christ Jesus had no such night of wrestling with God. There is no record in His life of long night in which God had to put His hand upon Him, and had to cripple Him for His defeat; His was the highest life; His was the life absolutely devoid of selfish desire, and not desire merely, but method. Jacob was seeking a Divine goal, but in his own; Christ sought the Divine goal in perpetual dependence on God. Can we too often reiterate this fact? There is nothing harder to get men to believe than this, that Jesus of Nazareth lived His life, and won the victory on the principle of faith in God. He distinctly said that He did nothing from Himself; He spoke no word from Himself; He ever waited for the Divine illumination, the Divine order; He walked for ever in the light of such Divine illumination, and obeyed for ever such Divine order; and therefore there was no period in his life where God had to break Him, so that He could win the victory in the full realization of his manhood.

And then, taking a further step, and speaking principally to young men and women here, I say to them there is no reason why you should have any such night of wrestling as Jacob had. I know that is not the ordinary and common conclusion to such a subject as this. I know we are very often told that every man must have his struggle at the Jabbok, and every man must receive the blessing of princely sonship after the process of believing. I do not believe it, I am perfectly sure that unless I find my way into the will of God without it then I must have my night of wrestling at the Jabbok, and I must be crippled to be a prince, but I do not believe that the higher Lord-life is the life that walks lame because it had to be crippled into royalty.

I have said so much of Christ, and it seems, perhaps, for a moment to have lifted out of the realm of possibility your own case, but may I remind you that Abraham had no such night of wrestling? He was the father of the faithful; he walked before God without questioning, refusing to choose when Lot made his choice, and God led him ever on toward the light of the city that was unseen. But, my brother, my sister, if I will not learn the lesson as Abraham learned it I must learn it as Jacob learned it. Sooner or later the crisis must come in my life in which I find out that although I outwitted Esau and am more keen than Laban, I must yield to God, and when I yield to Him and feel His strength upon me and hang upon it, the cry of my weakness is the cry of my victory. I do not know — this sermon tonight may be for one man. You may be in the midst of some crisis of life, some breaking crisis, and all your (you will forgive the word) conceit, your pride of will and pride of power, are ebbing away. My brother, the day breaketh. It is when you and I get there and we begin to feel that we cannot, that God looks into our faces and says, "No more Jacob, but Israel."

And now, watch. It is the last vision, no longer a night scene but a morning scene. "As he went through Penuel the sun rose upon him." And tonight as you pass from the dark, wrestling crisis of your life, in which it may be God cripples you, the sun will break upon you and you will call the name of that place, not "Bethel" merely "the house of God", but "Penuel", "The face of God"; and you will say: "I have seen Him face to face, and my life is healed by breaking; maimed by crippling, I am a prince, for God won, and in my defeat has come my triumph." Amen.

DOES THE NATION CONSIDER?

Isaiah 1:3

"My people doth not consider."

The early ministry of Isaiah was exercised in the later years of the reign of King Uzziah. Those were days of great material prosperity, and of marked spiritual degeneracy. The prophet understood the true spiritual conditions; and knowing whereunto they must inevitably lead, he spoke out of his sense of coming catastrophe. Thus his words were primarily for the days of national calamity. They are words which interpret national disaster. The central and fundamental truths are all found in the opening section of this truly remarkable book. Within the compass of the first chapter and the first five verses of chapter two, all the principles which presently are to be applied and to have fuller exposition, are revealed.

In the words I have taken as text, the Divine diagnosis of the situation is discovered: "My people doth not consider." Presently the prophet's revelation of the vantage ground of God in time of trouble is found: "Except the Lord of Hosts had left unto us a very small remnant, we should have been as Sodom." Further on we hear the Divine call through the prophet, not to the individual in the first place, but to the nation. "Come now, and let us reason together," saith the Lord; "though your sins be as scarlet, they shall be as white as snow." Finally, in the five opening verses of chapter two, we have the prophet's outlook upon the time of restoration, the great and golden day of peace that he saw shining through all the shadows.

As I have already said, our text constitutes the Divine diagnosis of the situation. In it the root of all subsequent trouble is revealed. All other things were symptomatic. The whole force of the statement is concentrated in the word "consider." The Hebrew word so translated means far more than "to think". The statement is not merely: My people do not think. It means rather that they do not think rightly; they do not come to true conclusions; they do not understand the actual facts of the case. Perhaps in our modern sense of another word we shall come nearer to understanding the declaration: My people doth not discern. Carlyle once said that the devil supremely hates the man who thinks. That depends. The Bible declares that God hates vain thoughts. That is a much profounder statement. There may be a great deal of thinking that gladdens the devil. The trouble with the people of God in the ancient time was not that they did not think, but that they did not discern. The thinking was not true; it did not lead them to true conclusions; while they thought that they had perfectly understood the times and the situation, they were really blind.

ISRAEL'S FAILURE TO UNDERSTAND ITS HISTORY

In our meditation let us follow two lines; first, considering the ancient story; and secondly, attempting a modern application. The measure in which our consideration of the ancient story is clear, will be the measure in which our modern application is really valuable. These people did not consider. They did not consider their history; they did not consider their prosperity; they did not consider their adversity. They failed to discern the truth concerning their history. They failed to understand the truth underlying the calamities that came to them. These are the obvious things in the story, and to them alone we give attention. They did not consider their own history. That history is summarized in the word of the prophet in which speaking on behalf of God, he said: "I have nourished and brought up children." It is the language of fatherhood, but it is immediately seen to be the language of One who claimed that the whole history of the people was the history of His dealing with them. The marginal rendering in the Revised Version may help us at this point: I have made great, and exalted, children who have rebelled against Me. The national life of this people was the outcome of Divine redemption. That was the continual burden of the Divine messengers. These people were constantly charged to remember that they were a ransomed people; that their nationality grew out of a Divine intervention, by which they were set free from slavery, and were brought to God, to be His peculiar possession. This people did not discern this truth concerning their history. They were interpreting their own history in another way. They were exalting great men and human successes. In the Apocrypha there is a chapter in celebration of great men. It is a very symtomatic chapter of the condition into which these people had come. They were exalting great men, and laying their emphasis upon the idea that their greatness resulted from the influence of these men and from their own clevernesses.

THE KING HELPED BY GOD

At this very hour this nation was trusting in policy and in power. Both the prophecy of Isaiah and that of Jeremiah reveal the fact that the politicians were at work attempting to arrange treaties and to make alliances in order to secure their safety. It was against that very thing that these men flung themselves with tremendous force and hot anger. Further, they did not consider their prosperity. The reign of Uzziah was one of wonderful prosperity. He overcame the Philistines that had so long harassed the nation, and so gave the people peace. But his work was not destructive only — it was constructive. He built towers in Jerusalem, and strengthened the city; he perfected the water supply; he secured agricultural prosperity; and he established a standing army. What was the secret of all this prosperity? That secret is revealed by two statements; God made him to prosper; and, he was marvelously helped. As a youth of sixteen years of age Uzziah was placed upon the throne, knowing his own weakness he sought God, and he was marvelously helped till he was strong. Uzziah's failure came not of his weakness but of his strength. All through the period of his conscious weakness, that early period of his wonderful reign, God made him to prosper. He was marvelously helped. Yet the people were attributing their prosperity to their own cleverness. The first eight chapters of Deuteronomy reveal the marvelous foresight of the great lawgiver, as before he left his people he delivered to them his great charges. He warned them against two things. He warned them that the day might come when they would say: Our own hand hath gotten us this wealth; forgetting that God gives man power to get wealth.

He warned them that the day would come when they would say: We are in this land because of our righteousness; forgetting that they were always a stiffnecked people, and that they were there only by an act of Divine grace. He solemnly charged them, moreover, that in the days of their prosperity they should never forget the strangers in their land, seeing that they themselves had also been strangers in a strange land. Their prosperity was not to be held for personal advantage, but in trust for all needy souls. Here had these people failed. They had not considered. They attributed their prosperity to their own cleverness, and were neglected of those in need. Yet once again, and finally in this glance at the old days, they did not understand their adversity. That is the meaning of these strange, wierd, and wailing questions:

> Why will ye be so stricken, that ye revolt more and more?
> The whole head is sick, and the whole heart faint.
> From the sole of the foot even unto the head there is no soundness in it; but wounds, and bruises, and festering sores; they have not been closed, neither bound up, neither mollified with oil.

That is a graphic and almost ghastly picture of the condition of the people in the day of adversity; bruised, battered, smeared with blood; and the question of God to them was this: Why will ye still have this kind of experience? One can almost imagine someone rising from the welter of agony and saying: Why will we have it? We do not desire it! Why does God continue it? But the real question for the nation in the hour of its calamity was not: Why does God do it; or, Why does God permit it; but, Why will ye have it so? They had not yet discerned the truth that this was chastisement, and they had not yet taken the true attitude of penitence in the presence of chastisement. They had not bowed their necks in the presence of God. They may even have suggested sometimes that perchance God was unjust in not delivering them from their calamity. They did not consider either their own history, or their prosperity, or their adversity; and out of that lack of spiritual intelligence proceeded all the other things which brought about the national ruin. So much for the ancient story.

ENGLAND DOES NOT CONSIDER

Now, secondly, for a modern application. Let me immediately say I am not proposing any discussion of the war, either as to its cause, its course, or its consummation. As a nation we are ranged on the side of righteousness and liberty. I make no apology for that declaration. We are far more certain of it, after a year, than we were at the beginning. The course and consummation of the war are under the control of God, and our relation to each other will be conditioned by our attitude to Him. I am now concerned with the national conscience, or perhaps I may say, with the national consciousness; or perhaps even better yet, with the national soul. There has been no public utterance during recent months more definitely prophetic than that of the Bishop of London on the great Day of Intercession, when amid the noise of uncertain sounds we heard a prophet of God speak of the national soul. It is that national soul in its consciousness of which I am thinking now. I propose to speak with all candor of things as I see them, and I declare that I think it is lamentably true that God may yet be saying of this nation: My people doth not consider. I am speaking of the nation. There are thousands of Godly men who are considering. There is a remnant. I propose to consider the fact of the value of the remnant in our next meditation. I am speaking now of the nation as a whole; and I declare it seems to me God may be saying to us: I have nourished and brought up children, but my people doth not consider, doth not discern. That I may not be unduly or improperly dogmatic I shall put what I have to say in the forms of questions.

Does the nation consider its history? What are the facts of our national history? Of the greatness of the Anglo-Saxon race there is no question. Personally I do not think the phrase, "Anglo-Saxon race," is an adequate one, yet we must employ it in the sense in which it is commonly used. Of the greatness of that race I say there is no question. But who are we, and whence came we? As to the first of these questions we must admit that we are an amalgam, and the amalgam is a very very strange one. We go back to the Ancient Britons. Who were they, and what were they? Julius Caesar declared that he found on this little island forty tribes. We profess to be able to trace some of their descendants until this time, and others, we know nothing about. It is an interesting thing, and sometimes, I think a profitable one, to remember how our four countries got their names. The only name that comes up out of antiquity is Ireland. The name of England was given to us by Teuton settlers here. That may chastise our souls a little. The name Scotland was given to the north land by Irishmen who settled there. The name Wales was an insult, meaning "Strangers", fastened on the Symri by the Saxons. All that is not very valuable, but if it helps us to see that when we ask who we are, we are at once in the presence of a difficulty, it is worth while. To the ancient stock there was a succession of intrusions: Roman, Saxon, Dane, Norman. When I proceed to the Whence came we of my enquiry, I am inclined in reply to quote from George Macdonald's poem on the baby:

Out of the everywhere into here.

That is the story of the nation, looked at so far as it is possible to look at in that way.

OUR SECRET: THE GOVERNANCE OF GOD

What then, is the secret of our national life? Not the genius of a race, for we are a strange and motley mixture. Not the foresight of a founder, for the founder is not to be found among the sons of men. But the governance — and that is a great word — the governance of God. I do not hesitate to state my own conviction superlatively, as I say that if in the Bible I have the story of how God made one nation, in the history of my own nation I have an equally wonderful, and in some senses more marvelous story of how God has made a second nation. Mark the things of our greatness at the present moment. I see three which greatly impress me. First, the law of our freedom; secondly, our colonizing genius; and thirdly, our Navy. Whence came the laws of our freedom that make us what we are? In the cloistered monastery, and not in the full consecrated monk, but in a serving many named Caedmon will be found the spring of the river. He began to put into the hands of the people parts of the Divine oracle. Next in the great procession there emerges King Alfred, truly called "the Great." Few men called great are really great, but he was.

Under him we find the first fashioning of our laws of freedom, and the very warp upon which the woof was built up was the Bible and the Biblical conceptions and ideals. So, away on, from the first singing of Caedmon, the serving-man in the monastery, ever struggling for victory with defeat, there emerges the greatness of our freedom. Is that the genius of a race? No! Is that the foresight of a founder? No! What is it? The governance of God.

Or think of the second thing that I have chosen to speak of as revealing our greatness — our colonizing genius. However much some men were inclined to deny this a year ago, they cannot do so now. There has been no more marvelous thing emerging in this cataclysmic year, than the revelation of the wonderful power of this people in the far-flung splendors of our Empire. What has been the secret of it? The very amalgam that constitutes our race, instructed in Biblical conceptions; the very fact that we are not one race with narrow prejudices attempting to force its conceptions upon other nations; but that we are a people finding natural sympathy with others, and ever bringing to them this same national conception of liberty. Our Colonial greatness is the result of God saying to us, as He said to Israel: I have nourished and brought up children.

A GREATER THAN DRAKE!

And finally our Navy. Why refer to it? Because to my mind it is the one great symbol of our strength in the material and physical realm. Whence came it? It is the child of Drake! Is it! I am a little tired of hearing about our glorious victory over the Spanish Armada. We won no victory over the Spanish Armada.

If it had not been for God's wind there would have been no victory. He broke the power of the Spanish Armada by the sweeping winds that drove them to their destruction. Out of that deliverance there came that great shield of the nation. Lord Rosebery told us last week that we were unprepared for war. I deny it absolutely. We were prepared within the limits of proper defense. We were not prepared, thank God, for anything in the way of aggression. But the greatness of this country today, as it is symbolized in the lowest level of the material, is the direct result of the governance and over-ruling of God.

Have we not also been glorying in men? Have we not also been vaunting ourselves? Have we not also been in danger of trusting in our own policies and our own powers? I leave these things as questions. Let me ask another. Does the nation consider its prosperity? Does it understand it? The great prosperity of recent years is undeniable. I call to mind, and have done many times during the past twelve months, a conversation I had fully twelve, perhaps more, years ago in the United States with a leader of thought. He then said that Great Britain was the most wealthy nation in the world. I denied it. Then he said: If ever, unfortunately, you should be involved as a nation in a great war, you will find out what your wealth is. Is it not true? The wealth of this country as demonstrated, speaks of the prosperity of the nation. Have we discerned the meaning of this wealth? Have we as a nation recognized that God gives us power to get wealth? Have we not said exactly what Moses said those people would say: Our own hands have gotten us this wealth. More! Have we not been in danger; nay, have we not been definitely guilty of the sin of selfishness in the past days of wealth? I leave these things also as questions.

DO WE CONSIDER OUR ADVERSITY?

I ask my last question. I do it with great care, you will believe me, with a sob in my heart if not in my voice. Does this nation discern, consider, understand its adversity? By adversity I do not mean defeat. I do not mean danger of defeat. I mean the patent fact, which has become so much more patent as the months run on, that we are sorely stricken. Already it is difficult to talk to anyone who is not involved in the suffering and the sorrows, in the loss and the agony of this welter of war. We are stricken people, I will not argue about it. It is granted. Then I ask my question. Is there any national consciousness of sin? Is there any national turning to God? When a distinguished woman of another nation comes to London she is amazed at London's light and frivolous laughter. There may be some answer to her amazement, a great and reverent answer. We may say to her that underneath the laughter there may be much agony of soul. And yet, so help me God, I see no sign of national repentance or national understanding that these are chastisements of God.

I declare to you today that it seems to me that the one supreme and overwhelming need, so far as the nation is concerned, is the need for a national repentance which finds its expression first of all in a recognition of God; then in the consecration of life and purpose to God; and then in the subdued and chastened spirit that accepts calamity as chastisement, and earnestly desires and strives to profit by the painful discipline.

How is this to be brought about in the life of the nation? There is a sense in which that question can only be answered by God. He is able to make His appeal to the nation in ways we know not, and we can pray that thus it surely will be. But it is equally true that the Church ought to be His messenger, and the most saddening outlook to me at this moment is the Church's inability to speak with unanimous authority.

Therefore today we leave our consideration. We shall resume it on Sunday morning next, when, God willing, we shall attempt to understand the meaning and value of the Remnant, through whom the nation shall be saved.

THE REMNANT OF GOD'S PEOPLE

Isaiah 1:9

"Except the Lord of Hosts had left unto us a very small remnant, we should have been as Sodom, we should have been like unto Gomorrah."

In our previous meditation we considered the Divine diagnosis of National Failure as it was expressed in the declaration, My people doth not consider — observing their failure to consider or to discern the truth concerning their history, their prosperity, their adversity. They lacked spiritual perception; they failed to take account of God. We now turn our attention to the prophet's revelation of God's vantage ground in such a time of degeneracy and failure. It consisted of what he described as a very small remnant. Because such a remnant existed, the nation was saved from becoming as Sodom and Gomorrah. That remnant saved the nation morally and judicially. Because of its existence the people never sank to the level of Sodom's corruption, and consequently the catastrophe of utter extermination never fell upon it. To the strengthening of that remnant Isaiah devoted a large part of his ministry.

This is the revelation of a principle of perpetual application. It runs through all Bible history. The first illustration of it in the Divine oracles is a very superlative one, and to that illustration the prophet himself referred by the figure of speech he employed in the text, and in that paragraph which immediately follows the text: "Except the Lord of Hosts had left unto us a very small remnant, we should have been as Sodom, we should have been like unto Gomorrah."

THE "REMNANT" IN BIBLICAL PROPHECY

It is evident that his mind was going back to the story of the destruction of Sodom and Gomorrah, because Sodom and Gomorrah lacked a remnant. That matchless picture is full of local color, and yet is full of eternal light. One man is seen communing with God — to employ the actual closing word of the narrative — about a city, in the interest of the righteous, pressing further and further in his argument with God on behalf of such. God is revealed as listening to him, bearing with him, admitting all his arguments, agreeing with him. Yet, at the last, as we know, the city perished for lack of a remnant.

The principle, as I say, runs on all through the Bible. The prophets were constantly addressing themselves to the remnant and insisting upon the importance thereof. The very words they employed to describe the remnant are most suggestive. There are at least five of them, and each is suggestive. I will do no more than name the suggestions. There is one which means a Remainder, in the sense of that which has escaped corruption, something which has lived in spite of prevailing death. There is another which means a Remnant, in the sense of those that are escaped from slavery and are breathing the air of freedom. There is another which describes a Residue, in the sense of those who retain excellence in spite of deterioration. There is yet another which describes a Refugee company who have left a region of desolation. And in the text we have a word which is only found here, and once again in the Prophecy of Joel, which really describes a survivor who has squeezed through a narrow opening into liberty, and alone is left, living and free.

Without following that further, I think you will agree that these words are a wonderful revelation of what the remnant really is. God's vantage ground is always created by a remnant; by such souls as fulfil in their own experience the suggestions of these words. Wherever there has been such a remnant, city, nation, people have been delivered from destruction. This principle of the remnant marked the method of Christ in the days of His public ministry. He made no national appeal, He made no political appeal. He gathered a remnant. His method was the most severe. We often dwell upon the tenderness of Christ and rightly so; we often emphasize the universality of His call to humanity, and with great accuracy. Yet it is impossible to follow Him through the pathway of His ministry without seeing that He was always far more anxious about quality than quantity; calling men to discipleship with a note of universal love, and as they approached Him holding them back, sifting their ranks uttering terms of discipleship most stern and severe; and all in order that He might have a gathered out people of high qualifications; a remnant, through which it might be possible to save the nation, and save the world.

THE CENTRAL PRINCIPLE OF THE CHURCH

This principle of the remnant is indeed the central principle of the life of the Church. In the life of the nation today, the Church of God should constitute a remnant which saves the nation from destruction. In God's universal economy, in the olden time, Israel was intended to be God's remnant, the whole people God's remnant in the midst of widespread corruption. He called a nation, and made it a nation peculiar to Himself in order that they might be His vantage ground for saving all the nations. In the great hour of communion between Himself and Abraham we have the record of God's thought, as He said: "Shall I hide this thing from Abraham, seeing that I shall make of him a great nation, and in him all the nations of the earth shall be blessed?"

As we follow the history of this people within the Old Testament Scriptures we discover that when they failed to fulfil the ideal, He found a remnant within their borders, and dealt with that remnant. I said a few moments ago that Isaiah devoted a large part of his ministry to the remnant. If we study this great prophecy with care we discover the very point at which he broke with the nation, and gave himself up to a remnant of elect souls under the Divine command. In the eighth chapter we find the word: "Bind thou up the testimony, seal the law among My disciples." That was the command. Following are the words of the prophet's obedience; "And I will wait for the Lord, that hideth His face from the house of Jacob, and I will look for Him. Behold, I and the children whom the Lord hath given me are for signs and for wonders in Israel from the Lord of hosts, which dwelleth in Mount Zion." When Ahaz refused his teaching, Isaiah left the king and left the court, and left the nation, and devoted his ministry to that circle of elect souls which were true to God in the midst of tribulation and corruption. He was strengthening the remnant, he was maintaining God's vantage ground, with the result that undoubtedly the kingdom of Judah was preserved for a hundred years longer than it would have been. At last, when Judah was itself destroyed, and its sons and daughters driven into captivity, God maintained His remnant, growing ever smaller, until in the fulness of time it became — to quote from Paul — not seeds as many, but a seed, one — Christ Himself. Today the Church, in the natural order of the Divine economy, constitutes God's remnant.

WHEN THE ORGANIZED CHURCH FAILS

Now, if the organized Church fails, God will find His remnant within her borders, a remnant of souls constituting His vantage ground, creating the possibility of the operation of His grace for the saving of the nation from ultimate corruption and so from ultimate destruction. What, then, are the characteristics of the remnant? The answer may be given immediately and inclusively by declaring that the remnant stands in absolute and complete contrast to Sodom and Gomorrah, that is, to Sodom and Gomorrah as realized in the chosen people.

Observe that in my text the prophet said: "Except the Lord of Hosts had left unto us a very small remnant, we should have been as Sodom, we should have been like unto Gomorrah." And then immediately he began to speak of Sodom and Gomorrah. "Hear the word of the Lord, ye rulers of Sodom; give ear unto the law of our God, ye people of Gomorrah."

It is self-evident that at this point the prophet was addressing, not the remnant, but the whole nation, and with a fine and searching satire he addressed that nation, the chosen nation which had failed to be God's remnant for grace, as Sodom, as Gomorrah. He addressed the rulers of the people as "the rulers of Sodom." He addressed the people themselves as "the people of Gomorrah." There emerges immediately the intended contrast between the very small remnant and the rest of the nation. The rest of the nation had become like Sodom and like Gomorrah. The prophet ignored their privilege, took no account of their position as the chosen people, but addressed them directly and immediately as Sodom and as Gomorrah. In his words immediately following we discover the spiritual condition of Sodom and Gomorrah, and so by contrast we discover the true nature of the remnant.

Let us attempt then to see Sodom and Gomorrah as here interpreted, in order that we may see the remnant as it must be, if it is to be God's vantage ground in such an age of darkness.

THE DOOM OF SODOM

The picture of Sodom here is the picture of a people spiritually insensate, ceremonially degenerate and morally polluted. I say first we have a people spiritually insensate. Notice his word: "Hear the word of the Lord, ye rulers of Sodom; give ear unto the law of our God, ye people of Gomorrah." The rulers were deaf to the teaching of God. They were deaf to the supreme voice, insensate to the profoundest facts of life. The rulers were listening. They were listening to the thunder of the approaching hosts beyond the confines of the nation; they were listening to the voices of the politicians within who were attempting to arrange treaties and alliances in order that they might be made safe; but they were not listening to God. The people were listening to the voices of their rulers, being persuaded, and swayed, and influenced by them; but they were not listening to the teaching of God. They were spiritually insensate.

Therefore they were ceremonially degenerate. The hour was characterized by elaborate religious observances. This we gather from the prophet's denunciatory words; a multitude of sacrifices, the holding of solemn assemblies, the offering of many prayers! It is probable that not for a long time in the history of Judah had there been more punctilious observance of all the external ceremonies of religion than in the days when Isaiah commenced his ministry. And yet God said of their offerings, "I am full of them." That is really so graphic a word that one is almost afraid to interpret it. In colloquial speech today we have a somewhat startling expression. Men say they are "fed up" with certain matters. It suggests absolute weariness amounting to disgust. That is what God said. I am tired of your sacrifices. I am full of them. I am fed up with them! Of their solemn assemblies God said, through the mouth of His prophet, I hate them! The reason is discovered in one revealing phrase — iniquity and the solemn meeting. There is nothing harmful in the solemn meeting. A solemn meeting is a thing of God! But not if there is iniquity there. Better no solemn assembly than a solemn assembly that lacks reality, truth, justice, purity.

Finally, in the presence of people with outstretched hands, and conventional prayers, God said — I will hide myself; I have no answer for these prayers. These are prayers that cannot be answered.

The result of spiritual deadness and ceremonial degeneracy is moral pollution. Everything is included in one statement: Your hands are full of blood! That should be interpreted by what follows. They had neglected judgment. The oppressed were not being relieved; the fatherless were being wronged; the widows were undefended. Lack of judgment always finally means lack of compassion, for judgment is the activity of compassion, and where there is no compassion there is no justice.

All that is background. "Except the Lord of Hosts had left unto us a very small remnant." That small remnant consisted of a company of men and women standing in complete and striking contrast to the condition of affairs in the midst of which they lived.

A PEOPLE SPIRITUALLY ACUTE

What then, are the true elements which constitute a remnant? A people spiritually acute; a people ceremonially honest; a people morally clean. Leaving the page of ancient story, and thinking now of the principle as it obtains at any time, and therefore today, we have a description of the remnant through which God can save any nation. They must be a people who are spiritually acute, a people who know God. This is an infinitely different matter from knowing about God. People who know God are people who find God everywhere; people who cannot get away from God, and have no desire to do so; people who understand the history of the nation of which they form a part, seeing it even in relation to the governance of God; people who rejoice in national prosperity, but always recognize that it is the gift of God; people who in an hour of calamity and sorrow recognize the chastisement of God, and set their faces in penitence toward the dust that they may lift them in confidence toward the light. Such people are not popular people. They never have been; they are not today. Their speech is a perpetual annoyance to all that is godless, however cultured and refined it may be. They talk about the will of God, and the world sneers; and the tragedy is that the Church too often sneers. They speak of God. They take an inventory of their wealth in Him; they cannot escape Him wherever they may be. I say their speech is a perpetual annoyance. Their activity is a constant rebuke. Their influence is that of salt and of light; salt, which holds corruption while it annoys the corrupt; light, which gives a chance to the man who is struggling towards the light, while it makes the lovers of darkness most angry. The remnant of God is, in the modern, and in the best sense of the word, a peculiar people.

HONESTY AND MORAL CLEANNESS

They are also ceremoniously honest. Their sacrifices are symbols and not performers. The song sung in the sanctuary is not meaningless. If they cannot sing the song honestly they will not sing. That is worship. Their assemblies are full of reality. When the remnant gathers together everything unnatural is destroyed by the passionate fervor of their loyalty to that which is true. Their prayers are sincere. When they say, "Thy will be done on earth as it is in heaven," they mean it. They break through conventionalities, they violate customs. Over and over again within organized religion, the remnant of God becomes an annoyance, because it will not conform. In that sense Jesus Christ was the supreme Nonconformist, violating the traditional observance of the Sabbath again and again of set purpose, in order to bring the nation back to a true sense of the sanctions of the Sabbath.

Given a remnant within a Church, any Church, it is possible that it may be excommunicated because it is not orderly. As a matter of fact, the members of such a remnant are the only orderly people in the Church. The fact of their devotion to honesty and their enforced breaking through conventionality, gives God His chance, which otherwise in the splendid regularity of the Church's failure He has lost and cannot find.

The Remnant constitute a people who are morally clean. They ascend unto the hill of the Lord — and now I shall continue the quotation — "with a clean hand and pure heart," for only one has ever done that, and that is Christ — they ascend unto the hill of the Lord with cleansed hands and purified hearts. They are people who gather at the table of the Lord, not to confess their sins, but having confessed them; they are people who come to worship on Sunday, not to get set right with God, but having been set right with God in the loneliness of their own communion with Him, that so their worship may be a worship of purity and strength. Morally clean, ascending the hill of the Lord with cleansed hands and purified hearts, and then descending into the valleys of life to exercise there on the holy compassion of true justice.

I do not propose any detailed application of this meditation. It carries its own message. A general statement will suffice. That there has been much of Sodom and Gomorrah in our national life must, I fear, be admitted. That the spirit of Sodom, and Gomorrah has invaded and infected the Church, I think none will deny. But, thank God, neither the nation nor the Church is like Sodom or Gomorrah, for God has His remnant. And there we leave the meditation.

WHO ARE THE "REMNANT"?

But in the light of it, we conclude by an inquiry, an inquiry which if expressed in the plural number only becomes finally dynamic, as it is asked in the singular number. Are we of the number of the remnant through which this nation can be saved? We may easily find out. The tests are before us. They are the very things we have been attempting to look at.

What of our spiritual sense? Do we discern, do we hear the voice of God, are we listening for that voice? Which are we the more anxious to hear? What God the Lord has to say, or what the Prime Minister has to say? You will not misinterpret that. I am among the number of those who believe that our one business in national affairs at this moment is to have implicit confidence in the Government. But we are all asking: What about the War? What does Lord Kitchener think about it? It would be very interesting to know, but absolutely unimportant. What does God think about it? Is that what we want to know? It ought to be. There is nothing of more vital importance today than that He should have in this nation today at least a remnant listening for Him.

Do we consider? Thank God there are thousands who are considering in this Empire today. There is a new quickening of spiritual sense everywhere. God has a remnant. Are we among the number?

What of our ceremonies — are they vain oblations? Is there not iniquity in our solemn assemblies? Is God saying of our very gifts, I am full of them?

The ultimate question is involved in those already asked. If God is saying of our gifts, I am full of them, weary of them for they are vain, they are empty, they are performances; if God is hating our gatherings together because they are unreal.

What of our morality? Are we clean? Are we

seeking to be clean? Nay are we constantly seeking cleansing? Are we going up into the hill of the Lord with cleansed hands and a purified heart?

Let us answer the question by asking another profoundly related to it. When we have been to the hill of the Lord, are we descending into the valleys of men inspired by a compassion that is seeking strict justice for the oppressed, for the fatherless, for the widow? You say, Is not that rather an ethical question? That is a religious question. That is the kind of question that God always asks when He comes for human examination. Are we clean? Are we holy? The answer is not to be found in our confessions, our professions, our songs, our prayers. The answer is discovered in our attitude toward need, toward agony, toward such as are oppressed, toward fatherless children, toward widows, toward all human suffering.

Let us remember how Paul interprets this doctrine of the remnant. He quotes my text in his Roman Letter, and instead of the word remnant he introduces the word "seed" thus reading into the thought of the word, the life principle and element. When writing to the Galatians, he says, using a profound distinction that has caused many expositors trouble: "Not of seeds as of many, but of seed as of one." The seed of the remnant is Christ. The remnant principle is at last reduced to the one, Christ, and so it is fulfilled.

The last question of all, then, is this: Are we Christians? Are we Christ's men, Christ's women? In proportion as it be so, and He is being realized within us by the Holy Ghost, in proportion as we are wholly yielded to the power of that Holy seed born within us; in that proportion we constitute His remnant. By that remnant the nation may be delivered. Amen.

CONSCIENCE

Tonight I have no text. If any one is sufficiently under the power of tradition to feel that a text is necessary, then either of the twenty-nine verses in the New Testament, in which the word "conscience" is found will serve, for Conscience is my theme. It would be even better to read all of them carefully, for this is what I have been doing this week in the preparation of this sermon.

Conscience is that at which some men mock, and if we could but know the truth, while they mock they feel the power of it in their own souls. Conscience is that in deference to which some men today in England are suffering imprisonment, and rather than disobey the dictates of which they are prepared to die.

The power of conscience has been recognized by philosophers, poets, prophets, and all great leaders of human thought. Shakespeare expresses it in the words of Hamlet: —

... The dread of something after death,
The undiscover'd country, from whose bourne
No traveler returns, puzzles the will;
And makes us rather bear those ills we have
Than fly to others that we know not of.
Thus conscience does make cowards of us all;
And thus the native hue of resolution
Is sicklied o'er with the pale cast of thought!

Crabbe, in his "Struggles of Conscience," has these lines: —

Oh, Conscience, Conscience, man's most faithful friend,
Him canst thou comfort, ease, relieve, defend;
But if he will thy friendly checks forego,
Thou art, Oh! woe for me, his deadliest foe!

Sterne, in "Tristram Shandy," says:—

> Trust that man in nothing who has not a conscience in everything.

George Washington, in his "Moral Maxims," wrote: —

> Labor to keep alive in your breast that little spark of celestial called conscience.

Or, once again, and perhaps in the whole realm of literature nothing is found more remarkable than the words of Byron: —

> Yet still there whispers the small voice within,
> Heard through gain's silence, and o'er glory's din;
> Whatever creed be taught, or land be trod,
> Man's conscience is the oracle of God.

What, then, is conscience? What is its value? What part does it play in life? How much heed ought we to pay to it? These and many other related questions are being forced upon us in this strange hour in which many things we have held as sacred are being postponed to a more convenient season. It goes without saying that in this pulpit, if we discuss the theme, it is in order that we may seek the Biblical light thereupon, and to that I may add that our discussion will be concerned with the truth itself rather than with any immediate application thereof.

THE BIBLE ON CONSCIENCE

As to the Biblical light, I shall begin by making some general statements. First, the word conscience is not found in the Old Testament, but the literature is full of the story of the operations of conscience in the human soul. Every record of a moral heroism is evidently the answer of a man to the call of his conscience. Every manifestation of immoral anger is produced by the activity of conscience. All the sobs of the penitent and all the songs of the forgiven are inspired by the working of conscience.

But the word is found in the New Testament. Presently we shall discuss it. For the moment let us note some general things concerning its use there. According to the New Testament, conscience "bears witness," "gives testimony," produces action, for things are done "for conscience' sake." In the New Testament conscience is described as "good" as "void of offence," as "pure," as "toward God." But conscience is also described in the New Testament as "weak," as "seared," or more literally, branded with a hot iron; as "defiled," as "evil". Finally, the New Testament declares that conscience can be "cleansed."

There is no clear-cut definition of conscience in the Bible. Perhaps the passages which come nearest to definition are two. The First is to be found in the Old Testament, "The spirit of man is the lamp of the Lord searching all the inward parts of the belly." In the New Testament the passage which always seems to me to come nearest to a definition of conscience occurs in the prologue to the Gospel of John, "The true light . . . . which lighteth every man." The spirit of man has many qualities, many quantities, many capacities, many activities. Among the rest it is in itself the lamp of the Lord. There is in every man a light shining.

Let us, then, consider, first, conscience in itself; secondly, conscience as to its place and power in personality; thirdly and finally, conscience as to its place and power in society.

"KNOWLEDGE WITH" — WHAT?

Our word conscience is almost a transliteration of the Latin word from which it is derived, conscientia, which simply means, knowledge with.

That definition, which is perfectly accurate and perfectly justified, and beyond which in some senses we shall not be able to go, leaves us asking questions. The suggestion of the word is evidently that of agreement. Necessarily the next question is: Knowledge with whom or with what? A writer on this matter of conscience has recently said: —

> The original connotation of the word implies a common agreement, a social idea shared by the community.

Is that so? I think not. There is absolutely nothing in the history of the word to warrant the impression that conscience means a social idea shared by the community, and there is certainly nothing in Biblical use to warrant it. Conscience is ever referred to in a peculiarly individualistic sense; it is personal, it is lonely.

Therefore we ask again: What is the suggestion of the word? If it be individual, if it be personal, if it be lonely, how can it be knowledge or conviction with? The answer is that the agreement suggested is that between a man's understanding and the fact he understands. Certain standards are postulated. Use what terms you will to describe them. Speak with the old philosophers of the reason, the idea, the essential and eternal truth; or speak in the language of religion, of the law, of ethics, of truth; conscience is the sense of the soul that apprehends those things. The knowledge is true, whether I apprehend it or not; but when I apprehend it, that is conscience.

In process of time the word has been reserved for

the moral realm, so that today almost invariably we draw a distinction between conscience and consciousness.

Conscience is the recognition of good and bad, the distinction between the right and the wrong — a distinction created, not by laws written outside the man which govern his life, but by the inherent sense of his soul in the presence of these things.

But conscience in the Biblical sense is far more than that. Conscience, normally, is always a warning against the bad, and an urging toward the good. Conscience is that activity of the human soul which recognizes the difference between goodness and badness, which makes the distinction quite clearly to the soul itself, and which then inevitable urges the soul toward goodness and warns the soul from badness.

Of the actual New Testament word our word conscience is in every sense so trustworthy and accurate a translation that I need simply say to remind you what that word is and of the slight difference, which finally is no difference at all. It means seeing with, that is co-perception. Again, we have the supposition of agreement, and it always has a moral value, and the moral value is exactly the same as that to which we have been referring. So much for the words themselves as to their meaning and their use.

CONSCIENCE'S NORMAL FUNCTION

Now as to the fact. Conscience is an activity of the human spirit in the moral realm, and normally it is wholly beneficent. Conscience is that within the soul of man which reveals goodness as goodness, which reveals badness as badness. Conscience is that which calls things by their right name; refuses to allow any evil thing to be re-baptized by a name that robs it of its meaning and significance. Conscience will call a lie a lie, and will not allow a man to escape by applying to it the high-sounding name of hyperbole. Conscience cannot prevent a man saying the untrue thing, but it will trouble him. It cannot prevent him saying it, but it does prevent him thinking it. No liar escapes that voice. He can become so accustomed to it as to laugh at it. That is the ultimate tragedy. Nevertheless, conscience persists. It is always unveiling the truth, always unmasking a lie, for ever warning the soul against the wrong of wrong, and the peril of wrong. That is the terror of conscience. But it is always luring the soul toward the high and the noble and the true, always inspiring the soul to follow the light, to follow the gleam, to obey the truth. That is the hope of conscience.

Conscience is an activity inherent in man by Divine creation, and active under Divine activity. This is the Biblical teaching from first to last in the Old Testament, where the word is never found, but the idea prevails; through the New Testament, where the word occurs, and the idea is even more powerful. God never leaves a man alone in this world. That may be challenged I know. Well, then, if it be true, as some theologians have taught, that there is a line over which a man may pass in this world, having crossed which there is no hope for him, if it be true that a man can in this life cross such border line, and be as hopelessly lost as though he had reached the darkling void where God is not, if that be true — I do not admit it — but if it be true, then remember that a man so abandoned of God has no conscience; he has no trouble about his sin, no pain of heart in the presence of it, no sense of the badness of badness. That agony of soul that is almost despair, when alone a man thinks of sin, is the touch of God in infinite mercy upon the soul of man. That is conscience. Conscience is infinitely more, and, I am inclined to say, infinitely other than a moral sentinel threatening a man with damnation. It will do that also. But why? In order to turn him back from the darkness toward which he is proceeding. The severer the voice of conscience the more terrific its appeal, the more poignant the agony of soul, the more sure is the evidence of the unfathomable and unutterable love of God. The very agony of conscience is a call of love.

A CAPACITY AND A RESPONSIBILITY

Some souls may be inquiring, Is it not so that the call of conscience does cease? Is it not so that there are men today who do not hear the voice? Are we not to gather from the manner and method of their lives that they hear no voice? I do not think we have any right to make a deduction. I believe that in the apparently insensate and depraved man the deepest thing is constantly a desire to escape from the infamy and shame. I give it to you as a private opinion, and I am quite willing to say I have not this on apostolic authority, but it is my profound conviction, after having come into personal contact with hundreds and thousands of men, that God does not abandon men in this world: "The spirit of man is the lamp of the Lord." The spirit of a man — the essential thing of him, that in which are resident all the capacities of his mind, his intellect, his emotion, and his will; that marvelous and majestic mystery of personality — God has so made it that it is His own lamp, His own light, the capacity for the appreciation of the goodness of the good, and of the badness of the bad, a perpetual warning against evil, and a constant urging toward good.

Therefore conscience is a capacity creating responsibility. Its warnings must be heeded, its promptings must be obeyed, or else it is weakened; it does not act with the readiness it once did; It becomes seared, branded with a hot iron, not sensitive to every movement in the spiritual world; it is defiled, and at last it is made utterly evil. Only as men obey conscience can they escape from perils that are suggested by these words of the New Testament.

CONSCIENCE IN PERSONALITY

Now as to the place and power of conscience in personality. All I have already been saying is pertinent at this point. Conscience exists in every human being, and originally it is good, pure, without offense, God-governed. In every little child conscience is good, conscience is pure, conscience is without offense, conscience is God-governed. The terror and the agony of things is that before the child has grown up our methods and habits of training and example too often spoil the conscience. But take a child naturally. I mean any child; that little child born in the slum; born in the East End slum, with all its squarlor and its filth, where the street is the only playground; or born in the West End slum, which is all veneer and false refinement and godlessness. Wherever the child is born, in that child spiritually the conscience is good, pure, without offense, God-governed.

The first exercise of conscience, of the normal conscience, is that of witnessing. It is that activity within the man, the woman, within youth, the maiden, the child, which is wholly personal. Yet the soul knows that it is somehow other than personal. Have you never sat down in the presence of some temptation, opportunity, duty, responsibility, and talked to yourself? Oh, no; I am not speaking now of muttering aloud, which is a sign of old age creeping on! I am thinking of something far profounder. I am thinking of the moment when you think all by yourself, and you first say: Yes, that thing is wrong; and then you say: I do not really see that it is wrong. Then, still alone, you argue with yourself. That is conscience; it is you. Ah, but "the spirit of a man is the lamp of the Lord"; that is also God — God dealing with you. That is the first activity of conscience, witnessing to the difference between good and bad, and always urging the soul toward the wrong. Later on, when we have disobeyed the voice, when we have not followed the gleam, when we have refused to walk in the light, when knowing the good we have chosen the bad, then conscience still witnesses within the soul, still emphasizes the difference, but now the supreme note of conscience is that of the condemnation of the wrong thing done. That is the haunting of conscience. The fame of Jesus spread over Galilee and Judea, and there was a man on a throne who said: It is John, whom I beheaded, risen from the dead! What was the matter with that man? He was Idumean; he was a Sadducee; he did not believe in resurrection. Ah, did he not? Conscience never let him escape from the wrong thing he had done, never allowed him to dodge the truth, that in a drunken debauch, to please a wanton woman, he had violated conscience. Conscience violated, wronged, battered, kept on, and when he heard that there was another Voice sounding, he said: It is John, whom I beheaded, risen from the dead. That is a wholly beneficent activity, that is still God in the soul; and had Herod repented, Herod had been ransomed and redeemed. Conscience is always calling men back. Consequently the first human responsibility in the matter of conscience is that of obedience, immediate, utter and at all costs.

THE CORRECTION OF CONSCIENCE

Yet there is another phase of responsibility. It is not enough that I shall obey my conscience. I must constantly seek the correction and re-adjustment of my conscience. Conscience may be weakened, conscience may be seared, conscience may be defiled, conscience may have become permeated and saturated with evil. Hence the necessity for the perpetual correction and readjustment of conscience. The light must be sought which comes from God Himself in order that I may know whether the light that is in me — to use the marvelous word of Jesus — be darkness or no. Conscience may be out of gear, may lead a man astray. Who shall correct it? Not you; not I; no human being can do it; God alone is able to do it. I well remember crossing the Atlantic once without a gleam of sunshine from the first moment to the last. As we were nearing New York the captain said to me: "We have been going by dead reckoning, and we are a little bit out of our course. We have had no sun, and all our mathematical precision breaks down unless the sun shines." That is the whole point. You come late to business, my dear young friend. I don't suppose you do; that is quite an impersonal remark. But let us suppose. You come late to business, and the person in oversight of your work says: "You are late." You reply: "You will excuse me, I am not late; it wants a minute to nine." The sharp reply is: "Your watch is wrong." Ah, yes! You must re-adjust your watch by Big Ben. Is that enough? No; Big Ben must be re-adjusted by Greenwich. Is that enough? It is if you remember that Greenwich is governed by the sun. Your conscience may get out of gear; it may be wrong. This is the most solemn consideration that every man ought to face in this particular hour. Your conscience may be misleading you. It may need re-adjustment, correction. John in his prologue referred to conscience when he said: "The light that lighteth every man"; and of it he declared, looking at Jesus: "There was the true light which lighteth every man coming into the world." He came that men might re-adjust the instrument of conscience by submitting themselves to His measurement, and His government, and His interpretation. That re-adjustment is a solemn responsibility. Prejudice must be denied. Pride must be impossible. Persistently, with regularity, sincerity and determination, conscience must be remitted to the Son, to the essential Light, to the Light beyond which there is no light, to the authority beyond which there is no authority, to the God who is good, and from whom the spirit of man proceeds. That spirit, which is His candle, must be held in His light, that a man may know whether or not his conscience is leading him astray. That is the human responsibility about conscience.

THE PLACE OF CONSCIENCE IN SOCIETY

And so, finally, what is the place and power of conscience in society? If all consciences were normal—

that is, good, pure, without offense, God-governed — there would be no difficulty in the matter of conscience. The conscience of each would be the conscience of all, and life would be a perfect harmony, and that is what it will be when God has finished His work with the race and completed His victory. But it is not so today. There are seared, defiled, evil consciences in the world. There are also weak consciences, and these are in the majority. Weak consciences are such as are not clear in their apprehensions of good and evil; they are not quick to discern. To borrow that phrase from the prophecy of Isaiah, in which the prophet describing God's great Messiah, said of Him: "He shall be quick of understanding in the fear of the Lord"; and to me the whole genius of that Hebrew word is most perfectly expressed by Dr. George Adam Smith's translation, "He shall be keen of scent in the fear of the Lord." That is true conscience. Weak consciences are not keen of scent in the fear of the Lord; they are not quick of understanding in the fear of the Lord. Here is the cause of conflict and difficulty in the realm of conscience. Here is a man whose conscience says to him, I am bound today to enlist and fight. Here is a man who says, My understanding of the will of Jesus is that I cannot do it. Who is to judge? I declare to you that you cannot, and you have no right to do so. I declare to the man who says that his conscience forbids his fighting, that he has no business to impose that conviction upon the man who says that he must fight; and to the man who feels the tremendous obligation of the present hour—there are multitudes of them, men whom we honor in proportion as they are true men — must respect the man who cannot share their conviction. There can be no judgment.

"Judge not, that ye be not judged. For with what judgment ye judge, ye shall be judged." That is a very solemn and searching word of Christ! This whole Biblical conception of conscience teaches us first that there must be a respect for the individual conscience; and further, that no attempt must be made to impose the law of personal conscience upon other men.

CONSCIENCE AND REASON

There should, however, be on the part of every man who takes his stand upon conscience, at least ability to give a reason for the faith that inspires him. Even though he may not be able to persuade another, even though he have no right to try and compel another to stand where he stands, surely he should be able to give a reason for the faith that is in him. During the period of stress — I do not mean this war now, I mean all life as we know it — the period of human imperfection, the period during which the temporary and imperfect expedient of government by majority is in force; during that time minorities are to be respected. If history teaches anything, it teaches that in running centuries over and over and over again it has been proved that the minority was right and not the majority. I give it you as a personal conviction that in every commission that has considered a great question, from the time when then the commission sat in the days of Joshua, as to whether they should obey God or not, the minority report has been the correct one, and not the majority. The majority said, There is the land, and it is great and wonderful land, but we cannot take it; there are giants and walled cities! That was the majority report. The minority said, We see the giants and walled cities, but we see God. I come right away down from them until the very latest Royal Commission that comes to my mind, that on Divorce, and it is the same story of the rightness of minorities! At last that should give us pause. It is a great thing when the multitude is right, but I am never going to be persuaded that anything is right because the multitude says it is. There must be for evermore in the heart of men who believe in this Biblical revelation a respect for minorities.

THE LAST STAND OF LIFE

The conclusion, however, must be on the inficidual note in any such consideration. For every man the last stand of life is that of his personal conscience being cleansed and void of offense. If the taking of that stand shall bring that man into the place of suffering, then let him suffer. A man who for conscience sake suffers and whimpers calls in question the reality of his conscience. "For this is acceptable, if for conscience toward God a man .... suffereth wrongfully." Let the man who suffers for conscience know that in all probability, the whole conception of the Bible bearing witness, and all human experience bearing testimony, suffering is winning a victory for the principle for which he suffers.

So, whether this way or that way, we may be doubtful at the moment as to what the part of duty is, one thing only matters, and that is that every man shall be fully persuaded in his own mind as he stands before God. So may He who cleanses human conscience give to us the conscience which is good and pure and void of offense, that, having done all things, we may stand.

www.ingramcontent.com/pod-product-compliance
Lightning Source LLC
Chambersburg PA
CBHW070920180426
43192CB00038B/2101